SECURITIES

S E R

AN INTRODUCTION TO THE GILT STRIPS MARKET

PROFESSIONALISM | INTEGRITY | EXCELLENCE

AN INTRODUCTION TO THE GILT STRIPS MARKET

Moorad Choudhry

First published in 1999 in Great Britain by
Securities Institute (Services) Limited
Centurion House, 24 Monument Street
London EC3R 8AQ, England.

Written by Moorad Choudhry

ISBN: 1 84307 006 5
Second edition August 2001, first printed June 1999

Printed and bound in Great Britain by
Antony Rowe Ltd, Chippenham, Wiltshire.

To Derek Taylor (who knows a bit about the gilt market!)

CONTENTS

About the Author

Moorad Choudhry works in investment banking in the City of London. He was previously employed as a Gilt–Edged Market Maker and Treasury trader at ABN Amro Hoare Govett Sterling Bonds Limited and as a sterling proprietary trader at Hambros Bank Limited. He has also worked at the London Stock Exchange.

Moorad obtained an MA in Econometrics from Reading University and his MBA from Henley Management College.

Preface

The gilt strips market is a fairly recent development, trading in strips having begun only in December 1997. The introduction of strips was an important step towards creating a more competitive structure for the UK gilts market, following the introduction of gilt repo and other reforms designed to bring the market structure up–to–date. While strips trading has experienced fairly low volumes and hence relatively low liquidity in the short time since the start of trading, the medium– and long–term outlook must remain positive. It is realistic to expect an increase in liquidity as volumes are built up over time. The customer demand for strips is potentially very large, as the instruments are simple to understand and have a wide range of uses; moreover their properties make them attractive to a variety of customers.

The strips market represents an opportunity to enhance the performance of gilt and sterling portfolios by adding flexibility to risk management. The unique performance characteristics of strips make them attractive for a wide range of trading and portfolio optimisation strategies. The potential customer base for strips can range from domestic insurance and pension funds to international investors and leveraged investors such as hedge funds.

The text begins by describing zero–coupon bonds in general and the basis of bond markets, bond market mathematics and interest rate risk, before taking a more in–depth look at the gilt strips market in particular. There are also sections on the uses of strips, types of customers who invest in strips and regulatory and settlement issues. We also present an introduction to trading strategy. The main sources of statistical information used are the Bank of England, the Debt Management Office and Bloomberg.

This book is aimed at those with little or no previous understanding of or exposure to the bond markets in general and zero–coupon bonds in particular; however it investigates the subject to sufficient depth to be of some use to more experienced practitioners. It is primarily aimed at front office, middle office and back office banking and fund management staff who are involved to some extent in fixed interest markets. Others including corporate and local authority treasurers and risk management and legal department staff may also find the contents useful. Comments on the text are welcome and should be sent to the author care of Securities Institute Services Ltd.

Chapter 1

INTRODUCTION TO THE BOND MARKET

Gilt strips are United Kingdom government bond instruments, which form part of the wider debt capital markets. Before considering the strips market in particular, it is worth looking at the bond markets in general. The basic principles that apply to bonds are also relevant to strips, so these are considered before we look at strips in more detail. We will start with an introduction to bonds and the general features of the bond markets as a whole.

DEFINITION

A bond is a debt capital market instrument issued by a borrower who is then required to repay to the lender/investor the amount borrowed plus interest, over a specified period of time. It is different from bank debt in that it is tradeable in the secondary market. There are as many different types of bonds as there are different borrowing entities. The most common bond is the *conventional* (or *plain vanilla* or *bullet*) bond. This is a bond paying a regular (annual or semi-annual) fixed interest rate over a fixed period to maturity or redemption, with the return of *principal* (the par or nominal value of the bond) on the maturity date. All other bonds will be variations on this. We can now look in more detail at some important features of bonds.

TYPE OF BORROWER

A key feature of a bond is the nature of the issuer (borrower). The United Kingdom government issues bonds known as *Gilts*. As they are issued and guaranteed by the government, gilts are the highest quality bonds available in the sterling markets. Issuers of bonds fall into four distinct categories: sovereign governments and their agencies, local government authorities, supranational bodies such as the World Bank, and corporations. Within the corporate bond market there is a wide range of issuers, each with differing abilities to satisfy the contractual obligations that are part off the bonds they issue.

TERM TO MATURITY

The *term to maturity* of a bond is the number of years over which the issuer has promised to meet the conditions of the obligation. The *maturity* of a bond refers to the date that the debt will cease to exist, at which time the issuer will redeem the bond by paying out the principal to the bondholders. The practice in the market is often to refer simply to a bond's "term" or "maturity". The provisions under which a bond is issued may allow either the issuer or investor to alter a bond's term to maturity. The term to maturity is an important consideration in the make-up of a bond. It indicates the time period over which the bondholder can expect to receive the coupon payments and the number of years before the principal will be paid in full. The bond's *yield* also depends on the term to maturity. Finally, the price of a bond will fluctuate over its life as yields in the market change (yields change as general market interest rates change) and as it approaches maturity. As we will discover later, the *volatility* of a bond's price is dependent on its maturity; assuming other factors remain constant, the longer a bond's maturity the greater the price volatility resulting from a change in market yields.

PRINCIPAL AND COUPON RATE

The *principal* of a bond is the amount that the issuer agrees to repay the bondholder on the maturity date. This amount is also referred to as the *redemption value*, *maturity value*, *par value*, or *face amount*, or simply *par*. The coupon rate or nominal rate is the interest rate that the issuer agrees to pay each year. The annual amount of the interest payment made is called the coupon. The coupon rate multiplied by the principal of the bond provides the cash amount of the coupon. For example a bond with a 7% coupon rate and a principal of £1,000,000 will pay annual interest of £70,000. In the United Kingdom, United States and Japan the usual practice is for the issuer to pay the coupon in two semi-annual instalments. For bonds issued in European markets and the Eurobond market coupon payments are made annually. Occasionally one will encounter bonds that pay interest on a quarterly basis.

All bonds make periodic interest payments except for *zero-coupon bonds*. Strips are zero-coupon bonds. Gilt strips are UK government bonds where the coupon has been "stripped" from the bond and traded separately. Hence all the coupons and the final principal that made up the original bond will become zero-coupon bonds. These bonds allow a holder to realise interest by being sold substantially below their principal value. This is referred to as being sold at a *discount*. The bonds are redeemed at par, with the interest amount then being the difference between the principal value and the price at which the bond was sold.

Another type of bond makes floating-rate interest payments. Such bonds are known as *floating rate notes* and their coupon rates are reset periodically in line with a predetermined benchmark, such as an interest rate index.

BONDS WITH EMBEDDED OPTIONS

Some bonds include a provision in their offer particulars that gives either the bondholder and/or the issuer an option to enforce early redemption of the bond. The most common type of option embedded in a bond is a *call feature*. A call provision grants the issuer the right to redeem all or part of the debt before the specified maturity date. An issuing company may wish to include such a feature as it allows it to replace an old bond issue with a lower coupon rate issue if interest rates in the market have declined. As a call feature allows the issuer to change the maturity date of a bond it is considered harmful to the bondholder's interests; therefore the market price of the bond will reflect this. For example a call option is usually included in all asset-backed securities based on mortgages, for obvious reasons. A bond issue may also include a provision that allows the investor to change the maturity of the bond. This is known as a *put feature* and gives the bondholder the right to sell the bond back to the issuer at par on specified dates. The advantage to the bondholder is that if interest rates rise after the issue date, thus depressing the bond's value, the investor can realise par value by *putting* the bond back to the issuer. A *convertible* bond is an issue giving the bondholder the right to exchange the bond for a specified amount of shares (equity) in the issuing company. This feature allows the investor to take advantage of favourable movements in the price of the issuer's shares, and will make the bond more attractive to investors.

Financial Arithmetic

DISCOUNTING AND PRESENT VALUE

The principles of compound interest have long been used to illustrate that £1 received today is not the same as £1 received at a point in the future. Faced with a choice between receiving £1 today or £1 in one year's time we would not be indifferent, given a rate of interest of say, 10% per annum. Our choice would be between £1 today and £1 plus 10p - the interest on £1 for one year at 10% per annum. The further one goes into the future, the greater will be the requirement to be compensated for interest foregone, because of the effect of *compounding*. The notion that money has a time value is a basic concept in the analysis of financial instruments. Money has time value because of the opportunity to invest it at a rate of interest, and over time investments accrue interest on interest, which is compounding.

COMPOUNDING

In compounding we seek to find a future value given a present value, a time period and an interest rate. If £100 is invested today (at time t_0) at 10%, then one year later (t_1) the investor will have £100 x (1 + .10) = £110. If he leaves the capital and interest for another year he will have at the end of year 2 (t_2):

$$
\begin{aligned}
& £110 \times (1 + .10) \\
= \quad & £100 \times (1 + .10) \times (1 + .10) \\
= \quad & £100 \times (1 + .10)^2 \\
= \quad & £121
\end{aligned}
$$

The outcome of the process of compounding is the future value of the initial amount. Therefore we can use the following expression:

$$FV = PV\,(1+r)^n$$

(1.1)

where

FV	is the future value
PV	is initial outlay or *present value*
r	is the periodic rate of interest (expressed as a decimal)
n	is the number of periods for which the sum is invested.

Equation 1.1 assumes *annual compounding*. Where semi-annual or quarterly compounding takes place, the equation is modified as shown below.

DISCOUNTING

The future value relationship established above can be reversed to find the *present value* (PV) of a known future sum. The equation then becomes:

$$PV = \frac{FV}{(1 + r)^n}$$

(1.2)

Example 1.1

You wish to have £1000 in three years time, and can invest at 9%. How much do you need to invest now? To solve this we require the PV of £1000 received in three years time.

$$PV = \frac{1000}{(1+.09)^3}$$

$$= \frac{1000}{1.295} = £772.20$$

Essentially in Example 1.1 the prospective future value of £1,000 was multiplied by $\frac{1}{(1+0.09)^3}$

which is called the *discount factor*, and which we had to calculate.

Tables of these factors already exist, called discount tables or present value tables, showing the PV of £1 received after *n* years at *r* rate of interest.

Compounding More than Once a Year

When interest is compounded more than once a year, the formula for calculating present values must be modified, as shown below.

$$PV = \frac{C_n}{\left(1 + \frac{r}{m}\right)^{mn}}$$

(1.3)

where C_n is the cash flow at the end of year n, m is the number of times a year interest is compounded, and r is the rate of interest as before. Therefore the present value of £100 to be received at the end of year 3, at a rate of interest rate of 10% compounded quarterly, is:

$$PV = \frac{100}{\left(1 + \frac{.10}{4}\right)^{(4)(3)}}$$

$$= £74.36$$

Internal Rate of Return

The internal rate of return or yield for an investment is the discount rate that equates the present value of the expected cash flows (the *net present value* or NPV) to zero. Mathematically it is represented by the rate r such that:

$$\sum_{t=0}^{n}\left[\frac{C_t}{(1+r)^t}\right] = 0$$

(1.4)

where C_t is the cash flow for the period t, n is the last period in which a cash flow is expected, and Σ denotes the sum of discounted cash flows at the end of periods 0 through n. If the initial cash flow occurs at time 0, Equation 1.4 can be expressed as follows:

$$C_0 = \frac{C_1}{(1+r)} + \frac{C_2}{(1+r)^2} + \ldots\ldots + \frac{C_n}{(1+r)^n}$$

(1.5)

Thus r is the rate that discounts the stream of future cash flows (C_1 through C_n) to equal the initial outlay at time 0-C_0. We must therefore assume that the cash flows received subsequently are reinvested to realise the same rate of return as r. This is exactly the same assumption and theory behind that used to construct the yield to maturity equation, which we will illustrate later; in fact they are essentially measuring the same thing. Solving for the internal rate of return r cannot be found analytically and has to be found through numerical iteration, or using a computer or programmable calculator.

The internal rate of return forms an important part of project appraisal in industry, where it is used as a type of break-even rate of return. It is therefore much used in corporate finance.

The Fair Pricing of Conventional Bonds

The theoretical price of a financial instrument is equal to the present value of the expected cash flows from the instrument. A vanilla bond pays a fixed rate of interest (coupon) annually or semi-annually, or very rarely quarterly. The *fair price* of such a bond is given by the discounted present value of the total cash flow stream, using a market-determined discount rate for a bond of its maturity and class of issuer, and assuming semi-annual discounting, as shown in the expression in equation 1.6.

$$
\begin{aligned}
P &= \frac{C/2}{\left(1+\frac{1}{2}r\right)} + \frac{C/2}{\left(1+\frac{1}{2}r\right)^2} + \ldots\ldots + \frac{C/2}{\left(1+\frac{1}{2}r\right)^{2T-1}} + \frac{C/2}{\left(1+\frac{1}{2}r\right)^{2T}} + \frac{M}{\left(1+\frac{1}{2}r\right)^{2T}} \\
&= \sum_{t=1}^{2T} \frac{C/2}{\left(1+\frac{1}{2}r\right)^t} + \frac{M}{\left(1+\frac{1}{2}r\right)^{2T}} \\
&= \frac{C}{r}\left[1 - \frac{1}{\left(1+\frac{1}{2}r\right)^{2T}}\right] + \frac{M}{\left(1+\frac{1}{2}r\right)^{2T}}
\end{aligned}
$$

(1.6)

where

P	is the fair price of the bond
C	is the annual fixed coupon payment
M	is the par value of the bond (usually 100)
T	is the number of *complete* years to maturity
r	is the market-determined discount rate or required rate of return for the bond.

Equation 1.6 calculates the fair price on a coupon payment date, so that there is no *accrued interest* incorporated into the price. It also assumes that there is an even number of coupon payments dates remaining before maturity. If there is an odd number of coupon payment dates before maturity the formula in 1.6 becomes modified as shown in 1.7.

$$P = \frac{C}{r}\left[1 - \frac{1}{\left(1+\frac{1}{2}r\right)^{2T+1}}\right] + \frac{M}{\left(1+\frac{1}{2}r\right)^{2T+1}}$$

(1.7)

Example 1.2

Fair pricing of a UK Gilt, 9% Treasury 2008

C	=	£9.00 per £100 nominal
M	=	£100
T	=	10 years (that is, the settlement date used in calculation date is 13 October 1998)
r	=	4.98%

$$P = \frac{£9.00}{0.0498}\left\{1 - \frac{1}{\left[1+\frac{1}{2}(0.0498)\right]^{20}}\right\} + \frac{£100}{\left[1+\frac{1}{2}(0.0498)\right]^{20}}$$

$$= £70.2175 + £61.1463$$

$$= £131.3638$$

The fair price of the gilt is £131.3638, which is composed of the present value of the stream of coupon payments (£70.2175) and the present value of the return of the principal (£61.1463).

There also exist *perpetual* or *irredeemable* bonds which have no redemption date, so that interest on them is paid indefinitely. The fair price of such a bond is given from 1.8 by setting T = ∞, such that:

$$P = \frac{C}{r}$$

(1.8)

Clean and Dirty Bond Prices

In all major bond markets the convention is to quote price as a clean price. This is the price disregarding accrued interest. The price that is actually paid for the bond in the market is the *dirty price* (or *gross price*), which is the clean price plus accrued interest. In other words the accrued interest must be added to the quoted price to get the total consideration for the bond. Accrued interest compensates the seller of the bond for giving up all of the next coupon payment even though he will have held the bond for part of the period since the last coupon payment. The clean price for a bond will move with changes in market interest rates; assuming that this is constant in a coupon period, the clean price will be constant for this period. However the dirty price for the same bond will increase steadily from one interest payment date until the next one.

On the coupon date the clean and dirty prices are the same and the accrued interest is zero. Between the coupon payment date and the next *ex dividend* date the bond is traded *cum dividend*, so that the buyer gets the next coupon payment. The seller is compensated for not receiving the next coupon payment by receiving accrued interest instead. This is positive and increases up to the next ex dividend date, at which point the dirty price falls by the present value of the amount of the coupon payment. The dirty price at this point is below the clean price, reflecting the fact that accrued interest is now negative. This is because after the ex dividend date the bond is traded "ex dividend"; the seller not the buyer receives the next coupon and the buyer has to be compensated for not receiving the next coupon by means of a lower price for holding the bond.

As gilt strips are zero-coupon bonds there is no accrued interest and in fact they are traded on a yield rather than price basis, which we shall consider later.

Bond Yield Measurement

Bonds are generally traded on the basis of their prices but because of the complicated patterns of cash flows that different bonds can have, they are generally compared in terms of their yields. The yield on any investment is the interest rate that will make the present value of the cash flows from the investment equal to the cost (price) of the investment. Mathematically the yield on any investment, represented by r, is the interest rate that satisfies equation 1.9 below.

$$P = \sum_{t=1}^{n} \frac{C_t}{(1+r)^t}$$

(1.9)

where

C_t	is the cash flow in year t
P	is the price of the investment
n	is the number of years

YIELD TO MATURITY

The yield calculated from the relationship illustrated by 1.9 above is also known as the internal rate of return. The main measure of bond return used in the markets is the yield to maturity (also known as *redemption yield*). The equation for a bond yield to maturity is similar to 1.9 above and is shown below for a bond paying semi-annual coupons.

$$P_d = \left[\frac{1}{\left(1+\frac{1}{2}r\right)^{N_{tc}/182.5}}\right] \text{x} \left[C/2 + \frac{C/2}{\left(1+\frac{1}{2}r\right)} + \;....\; + \frac{C/2}{\left(1+\frac{1}{2}r\right)^{S-1}} + \frac{M}{\left(1+\frac{1}{2}r\right)^{S-1}}\right]$$

$$= \left[\frac{1}{\left(1+\frac{1}{2}r\right)^{N_{tc}/182.5}}\right] \text{x} \left[\sum_{t=0}^{S-1} \frac{C/2}{\left(1+\frac{1}{2}r\right)^{t}} + \frac{M}{\left(1+\frac{1}{2}r\right)^{S-1}}\right]$$

$$= \left[\frac{1}{\left(1+\frac{1}{2}r\right)^{N_{tc}/182.5}}\right] \text{x} \left\{\frac{C}{r}\left[\left(1+\frac{1}{2}r\right) - \frac{1}{\left(1+\frac{1}{2}r\right)^{S-1}}\right] + \frac{M}{\left(1+\frac{1}{2}r\right)^{S-1}}\right\}$$

(1.10)

where

P_d	is the dirty price of the bond
r	is the yield to maturity

N_{tc} is the number of days between the current date and the next coupon date

C is the coupon

M is the redemption payment (par value of the bond)

S is the number of coupon payments before redemption; if T is the number of complete years before redemption, then $S = 2T$ if there is an even number of coupon payments before redemption, and $S = 2T+1$ if there is an odd number of coupon payments before redemption

In fact, this is the equation for what is known as a bond's *consortium yield* (a type of redemption yield), the calculation for which assumes 182.5 days in each semi-annual coupon period; in other words, a 365-day year.

The yield to maturity is not the actual return that will be realised from holding a bond for any length of time, or even to maturity, but rather an *anticipated* yield. That is, at the time of purchase, whether on issue or subsequently, the bondholder is promised a yield as measured by the yield to maturity, if the following conditions are satisfied:

- the bond is held to maturity;
- all coupon interest payments are reinvested at the stated yield to maturity.

The yield to maturity measurement of bond return assumes that the above conditions are always met, and therefore it is only accurate under these assumptions. In practice they will not usually apply (certainly the assumption of uniform reinvestment rates throughout the life of a bond is unrealistic) and therefore the stated yield will not be realised.

In addition, as coupons are discounted at the yield specific for each bond, it actually becomes inaccurate to compare bonds using this yield measure. For instance the coupon cashflows that occur in two years time from both a two-year and five-year bond will be discounted at different rates (assuming we do not have a flat yield curve). This is clearly not correct because we can see that the present value of a cashflow in two years time should be the same whether it is sourced from a short- or long-dated bond. Even if the first condition noted above is satisfied, it is clearly unlikely for any but the shortest maturity bond that all coupons will be reinvested at the same rate. Market interest rates are in a state of constant flux and hence this would affect money reinvestment rates. Therefore although yield to maturity is the main market measure of bond levels, it is not a true interest rate. This is an important result and we shall explore the concept of a true interest rate later in the book.

The uncertainty surrounding what market interest rates will be when a coupon is paid is part of the risks involved in holding a bond; specifically it is known as *reinvestment risk*.

A zero-coupon bond does not pay any coupon and therefore the equation for its yield to maturity is slightly simplified. Considering that a zero-coupon bond has only one cash flow, its payment on redemption, the equation for its yield to maturity is:

$$P = \frac{C_n}{(1+r)^n}$$

(1.11)

Re-arranging for the yield measure r we have

$$r = \left(\frac{C_n}{P}\right)^{\frac{1}{n}} - 1$$

(1.12)

where

P	is the bond price
C_n	is the cash flow at n (in fact the redemption payment, or par [100])
n	is the number of years to redemption

HOLDING PERIOD RETURN

The *holding-period yield*, sometimes known as the *reinvestment yield* is the average yield realised during the period in which the bond is held, taking into account changes in the reinvestment rate (the interest rate at which coupon payments can be reinvested). The risk that the rollover rate is less than the bond's yield to maturity is the bond's reinvestment risk.

The holding-period yield rh (assuming that the bond is bought on a coupon date so that accrued interest is zero, and sold an even number of coupon payments later [so that T is an integer]) is calculated using expression 1.13 below.

$$rh = \left\{ \left[\frac{(C/2)(1+\frac{1}{2}r_1)^{2T-1} + \ .... \ + (C/2) + P_1}{P_d} \right]^{\frac{1}{2}T} - 1 \right\} \text{x } 2$$

(1.13)

where *ri* is the rollover rate of interest earned by the ith coupon payment and P_1 is the price at which the bond was sold.

RUNNING YIELD

A bond's *running* (or *current* or *flat yield*) is a simple yield measure that essentially calculates the interest earned; as such it is used to measure the cost or profit from holding a bond. For example, if the short-term money market rate is lower than a bond's running yield, there will be a positive gain. This is referred to as *positive funding* or *positive carry*. The running yield on a bond is given by 1.14 below.

$$rc = \frac{C}{P}$$

(1.14)

Chapter 2

ZERO–COUPON BONDS

Strips are zero–coupon bonds. That is, they are bonds with only a single cash flow, which is the redemption payment on maturity. As such they are *discount* instruments. In this section we review the origins of strips trading and briefly describe overseas markets. The name for zero–coupon bonds originated in the US Treasury market and is derived from the expression "***S**eparate **T**rading of **R**egistered **I**nterest and **P**rincipal **S**ecurities*", which was introduced officially by the US Treasury in 1985. This was first used to denote zero–coupon bonds constructed from conventional bonds in the US Treasury market. The term "strip" denoting a zero–coupon bond should not be confused with other instruments traded in the market that use the same term; specifically futures strips, which denote a position made up of futures contracts ranging along the maturity band; and a strip hedge, which is an interest rate hedging technique that involves a hedge position along various points of the yield curve, as opposed to using only one point of the curve.

Market Origins

Strips trading originated in the United States. The US Treasury, like the Bank of England (BoE), does not issue zero–coupon bonds. In 1982 two investment banks, Merrill Lynch and Salomon Brothers (now Schroders Salomon Smith Barney, part of Travelers Citigroup group) constructed synthetic zero–coupon Treasury receipts. Both banks did this by buying Treasury bonds and depositing them in a custodian account; they then issued receipts representing each of the coupon payments and one on the principal repayment. The process of separating coupons from the principal and selling paper against each cash flow was known as "coupon stripping". The receipts traded by the banks were not issued by the US Treasury, however the underlying bond, held in a safe–custody account, *was* guaranteed by the government. Therefore the cash flows represented by the receipts were considered secure and traded as US government debt.

We can illustrate the process in the US market as follows. Consider a $100 million Treasury bond with a 10–year maturity and a coupon of 8%; if this is purchased in order to construct zero–coupon bonds, the cash flows will be 20 semi–annual payments of $4 million each and a principal repayment of $100 million in 10 years time. The bond is deposited in a bank safe–custody account. The purchasing bank then issues receipts against each of the cash flows; as the Treasury will make 21 different payments during the life of the bond, 21 receipts will be issued, each representing a zero–coupon bond. The maturity date for each receipt, or strip, must match the coupon payment dates of the bond and the final maturity date. Initially different banks issued receipts with their own unique name (for example, Merrill Lynch strips were known as TIGRs for *Treasury Income Growth Receipts*) and for this reason the secondary market for these strips was fairly illiquid, as strips were not considered fungible. To increase liquidity, Treasury primary dealers instead issued receipts known as "Treasury Receipts" which represented ownership of a generic Treasury security, as opposed to a share of the specific bond held in custody by the issuing bank. Although this was an improvement, settlement at this stage was still by physical delivery which hindered liquidity.

The US Treasury and Federal Reserve initially did not support the practice of stripping, viewing it as a tax avoidance measure. Subsequent tax legislation removed any tax advantages from stripping. In February 1985 the Treasury announced the STRIPS programme, which allowed the stripping of designated government bonds. The programme states that all new Treasuries with maturities of ten years or more are eligible for stripping; furthermore zero–coupon bonds created as part of the programme remain direct obligations of the US government. The strips are settled, like conventional Treasury securities, within the Federal Reserve's book–entry system; this results in a liquid secondary market.

Strips were originally created by banks seeking to profit by arbitraging the pricing differences between conventional bonds and strips; while such mispricing and arbitrage opportunities are rare in a developed and liquid market, they still exist and we shall discuss these issues in a later section.

Strips in Overseas Markets

The previous section outlined the origins of strips in the US market. As is the case in the conventional government bond market, the US strips market is a large, liquid and active market. At the beginning of 1999 the market exceeded $250 billion nominal outstanding *(Source: Bloomberg)*. Strips also trade in other markets. For instance there is an active, efficient market in France, where zero–coupon bonds are created from eligible securities, all of which have 25 April and 25 October coupon dates. We will look briefly at two markets in Europe.

HOLLAND

The Dutch Treasury introduced stripping of government bonds ("DSLs") in February 1993. Strips may be created by dealers trading coupons separately from the principal; it is also possible to re–constitute a conventional bond by rejoining strips to a principal. As at December 1998 four bonds had been stripped, shown below, with nominal values in billions of guilders.

Bond	Amount in Issue	Stripped Amount
9% DSL 2001	13.5	0.1
5.75% DSL 2004	16.5	0.3
7.5% DSL 2023	18.1	5.3
5.5% DSL 2028	4.0	0.5

(Source: Business Techniques, 1998)

The total nominal value of strips outstanding at that time was NGL 6.2 billion.

GERMANY

The Bundesbank introduced strips to the Bund market in July 1997. To strip a bond, the dealer places the Bund into the book–entry settlement and custody system, the *Deutsche Kassenverein AG* (DKV) and receives back each cash flow as a separate security. Each security then trades as a strip. This process can be performed by all bond holders and not just bund market makers. Reconstituting a bond requires carrying out the opposite action in which the coupon strips and principal are exchanged in return for the actual bond. Reconstituting bunds can only be carried out by banks and non–domestic investors with links to the DKV. This can take place via the Cedel and Euroclear settlement systems.

Initially the set of strippable bunds consisted of four bonds, two ten–year and two thirty–year issues. Subsequently new issue ten–year and thirty–year benchmarks have been eligible. The principal strips trade in multiples of DEM 1000, while the coupon strips trade in multiples of DEM 1. Stripping and reconstituting takes place in multiples of DEM 100,000. As in the US market all coupon strips are *fungible*, so for example coupon strips of the 6.25% 2024 bund can be used to reconstitute the 6% 2007 bund.

Chapter 3

THE YIELD CURVE

The most commonly occurring yield curve is the *yield to maturity yield curve*. The curve itself is constructed by plotting the yield to maturity against the term to maturity for a group of bonds of the same class. Three hypothetical examples are shown at Figure 3.1. Bonds used in constructing the curve will only rarely have an exact number of whole years to redemption; however it is often common to see yields plotted against whole years on the x-axis. This is because once a bond is designated the *benchmark* for that term, it's yield is taken to be the representative yield. For example, the ten-year benchmark gilt during 1999, the 5¾% Treasury 2009, will maintain its benchmark status throughout 1999, even as it's term to maturity reduces to below ten years.

As we might expect, given the source data from which it is constructed, the yield to maturity yield curve contains some inaccuracies. We have already come across the main weakness of the yield to maturity, the assumption of a constant rate for coupons during the bond's life at the redemption yield level. Since market rates will fluctuate over time, it will not be possible to achieve this (a feature known as *reinvestment risk*). Only zero-coupon bondholders avoid reinvestment risk as no coupon is paid during the life of a zero-coupon bond.

The yield to maturity yield curve does not distinguish between different payment patterns that may result from bonds with different coupons, that is, the fact that low-coupon bonds pay a higher portion of their cash flows at a later date than high-coupon bonds of the same maturity. The yield to maturity yield curve assumes an even cash flow pattern for all bonds. Therefore in this case cash flows are not discounted at the appropriate rate for the bonds in the group being used to construct the curve. To get around this bond analysts may sometimes construct a *coupon yield curve*, which plots yield to maturity against term to maturity for a group of bonds with the same coupon. This may be useful when a group of bonds contains some with very high coupons; high coupon bonds often trade "cheap to the curve", that is they have higher yields, than corresponding bonds of same maturity but lower coupon. This is usually because of reinvestment risk and, in the UK market, for tax reasons.

For the reasons we have discussed the market often uses other types of yield curve for analysis when the yield to maturity yield curve is deemed unsuitable.

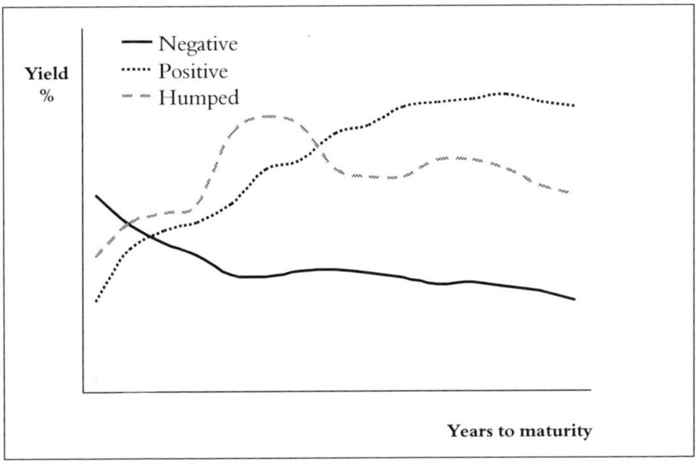

Fig 3.1 Yield to maturity yield curves

The par yield curve

The *par yield curve* is not usually encountered in secondary market trading, however it is often constructed for use by corporate financiers and others in the new issues or *primary* market. The par yield curve plots yield to maturity against term to maturity for current bonds trading at par. The par yield is therefore equal to the coupon rate for bonds priced at par or near to par, as the yield to maturity for bonds priced exactly at par is equal to the coupon rate. Those involved in the primary market will use a par yield curve to determine the required coupon for a new bond that is to be issued at par.

As an example consider for instance that par yields on one-year, two-year and three-year bonds are 5 per cent, 5.25 per cent and

5.75 per cent respectively. This implies that a new two-year bond would require a coupon of 5.25 per cent if it were to be issued at par; for a three-year bond with annual coupons trading at par, the following equality would be true:

$$100 = \frac{5.75}{1.0575} + \frac{5.75}{(1.0575)^2} + \frac{105.75}{(1.0575)^3}$$

This demonstrates that the yield to maturity and the coupon are identical when a bond is priced in the market at par.

The par yield curve can be derived directly from bond yields when bonds are trading at or near par. If bonds in the market are trading substantially away from par then the resulting curve will be distorted. It is then necessary to derive it by iteration from the spot yield curve.

The zero-coupon (or spot) yield curve

The *zero-coupon* (or *spot*) *yield curve* plots zero-coupon yields (or spot yields) against term to maturity.[1] In the first instance if there is a liquid zero-coupon bond market we can plot the yields from these bonds if we wish to construct this curve. However it is not necessary to have a set of zero-coupon bonds in order to construct this curve, as we can derive it from a coupon or par yield

---

[1] Although we have used the terms synonymously, strictly speaking they are not synonymous. A spot interest rate is a theoretical construct, and does not exist in practice. However as the definition of the spot rate is an interest rate chargeable to (or returned by) a single cash flow that is paid at some point in the future, the practical reality of a spot rate is the interest rate at which a zero-coupon bond of identical maturity is traded, which is why the two terms are often used interchangeably.

curve; in fact in markets where no zero-coupon bonds are traded, a spot yield curve is derived from the conventional yield to maturity yield curve. This of course would be a *theoretical* zero-coupon (spot) yield curve, as opposed to the *market* spot curve that can be constructed from yields of actual zero-coupon bonds trading in the market. We described the bootstrapping method of calculating spot rates in the previous section.

Spot yields must comply with equation 3.1, this equation assumes annual coupon payments and that the calculation is carried out on a coupon date so that accrued interest is zero.

$$P_d = \sum_{t=1}^{T} \frac{C}{(1+rs_t)^t} + \frac{M}{(1+rs_T)^T}$$

$$= \sum_{t=1}^{T} C \text{ x } D_t + M \text{ x } D_T$$

(3.1)

where

rs_t is the spot or zero-coupon yield on a bond with t years to maturity

$D_t \equiv$ $1/(1 + rs_t)^t$ = the corresponding *discount factor*

In 3.1, rs_1 is the current one-year spot yield, rs_2 the current two-year spot yield, and so on. Theoretically the spot yield for a particular term to maturity is the same as the yield on a zero-coupon bond of the same maturity, which is why spot yields are also known as *zero-coupon yields*.

As with the yield to redemption yield curve the spot yield curve is commonly used in the market. It is viewed as the true term structure of interest rates because there is no reinvestment risk involved; the stated yield is equal to the actual annual return. That is, the yield on a zero-coupon bond of *n* years maturity is regarded as the true n-year interest rate. Because the observed government bond redemption yield curve is not considered to be the true interest rate, analysts often construct a theoretical spot yield curve. Essentially this is done by breaking down each coupon bond into a series of zero-coupon issues. For example, £100 nominal of a 10 per cent two-year bond is considered equivalent to £10 nominal of a one-year zero-coupon bond and £110 nominal of a two-year zero-coupon bond.

Let us assume that in the market there are 30 bonds all paying annual coupons. The first bond has a maturity of one year, the second bond of two years, and so on out to thirty years. We know the price of each of these bonds, and we wish to determine what the prices imply about the market's estimate of future interest rates. We naturally expect interest rates to vary over time, but that all payments being made on the same date are valued using the same rate. For the one-year bond we know its current price and the amount of the payment (comprised of one coupon payment and the redemption proceeds) we will receive at the end of the year; therefore we can calculate the interest rate for the first year: assume the one-year bond has a coupon of 10 per cent. If we invest £100 today we will receive £110 in one year's time, hence the rate of interest is apparent and is 10 per cent. For the two-year bond we use this interest rate to calculate the future value of its current price in one year's time: *this is how much we would receive if we had invested the same amount in the one-year bond*. However the two-year bond pays a coupon at the end of the first year; if we subtract this amount from the future value of the current price, the net amount is what we should be giving up in one year in return for the one remaining payment. From these numbers we can calculate the interest rate in year two.

Assume that the two-year bond pays a coupon of 8 per cent and is priced at 95.00. If the 95.00 was invested at the rate we calculated for the one-year bond (10 per cent), it would accumulate £104.50 in one year, made up of the £95.00 investment and coupon interest of £9.50. On the payment date in one year's time, the one-year bond matures and the two-year bond pays a coupon of 8 per cent. If everyone expected that at this time the two-year bond would be priced at more than 96.50 (which is 104.50 minus 8.00), then no investor would buy the one-year bond, since it would be more advantageous to buy the two-year bond and sell it after one year for a greater return. Similarly if the price was less than 96.50 no investor would buy the two-year bond, as it would be cheaper to buy the shorter bond and then buy the longer-dated bond with the proceeds received when the one-year bond matures. Therefore the two-year bond must be priced at exactly 96.50 in 12 months time. For this £96.50 to grow to £108.00 (the maturity proceeds from the two-year bond, comprising the redemption payment and coupon interest), the interest rate in year two must be 11.92 per cent. We can check this using the present value formula covered earlier. At these two interest rates, the two bonds are said to be in *equilibrium*.

This is an important result and shows that there can be no arbitrage opportunity along the yield curve; using interest rates available today the return from buying the two-year bond must equal the return from buying the one-year bond and rolling over the proceeds (or *reinvesting*) for another year. This is the known as the *breakeven principle*.

Using the price and coupon of the three-year bond we can calculate the interest rate in year three in precisely the same way. Using each of the bonds in turn, we can link together the *implied one-year rates* for each year up to the maturity of the longest-dated bond. The process is known as *boot-strapping*. The "average" of the rates over a given period is the spot yield for that term: in the example given above, the rate in year one is 10 per cent, and in year two is 11.92 per cent. An investment of £100 at these rates would grow to £123.11. This gives a total percentage increase of 23.11 per cent over two years, or 10.956% per annum (the average rate is not obtained by simply dividing 23.11 by 2, but – using our present value relationship again – by calculating the square root of "1 plus the interest rate" and then subtracting 1 from this number). Thus the one-year yield is 10 per cent and the two-year yield is 10.956 per cent.

In real-world markets it is not necessarily as straightforward as this; for instance on some dates there may be several bonds maturing, with different coupons, and on some dates there may be no bonds maturing. It is most unlikely that there will be a regular spacing of redemptions exactly one year apart. For this reason it is common for practitioners to use a software model to calculate the set of implied forward rates which best fits the market prices of the bonds that do exist in the market. For instance if there are several one-year bonds, each of their prices may imply a slightly different rate of interest. We will choose the rate which gives the smallest average price error. In practice all bonds are used to find the rate in year one, all bonds with a term longer than one year are used to calculate the rate in year two, and so on. The zero-coupon curve can also be calculated directly from the par yield curve using a method similar to that described above; in this case the bonds would be priced at par (100.00) and their coupons set to the par yield values.

The zero-coupon yield curve is ideal to use when deriving implied forward rates and defining the term structure of interest rates. It is also the best curve to use when determining the relative value, whether cheap or dear, of bonds trading in the market, and when pricing new issues, irrespective of their coupons. However it is not an accurate indicator of average market yields because most bonds are not zero-coupon bonds.

The forward yield curve

The *forward* (or *forward-forward*) yield curve is a plot of forward rates against term to maturity. Forward rates satisfy expression 3.2 below.

$$P_d = \frac{C}{(1+{}_0rf_1)} + \frac{C}{(1+{}_0rf_1)(1+{}_1rf_2)} + \dots + \frac{M}{(1+{}_0rf_1)\dots(1+{}_{T-1}rf_T)}$$

$$= \sum_{t=1}^{T} \frac{C}{\prod_{i=1}^{t}(1+{}_{i-1}rf_i)} + \frac{M}{\prod_{i=1}^{T}(1+{}_{i-1}rf_i)}$$

(3.2)

where

$_{t-1}rf_t$ is the implicit forward rate (or forward-forward rate) on a one-year bond maturing in year t

Comparing 3.1 and 3.2 we can see that the spot yield is the *geometric mean* of the forward rates, as shown below.

$$(1+rs_t)^t = (1+{}_0rf_1)(1+{}_1rf_2)\ \ldots\ (1+{}_{t-1}rf_t)$$

(3.3)

This implies the following relationship between spot and forward rates:

$$(1+{}_{t-1}rf_t) = \frac{(1+rs_t)^t}{(1+rs_{t-1})^{t-1}}$$

$$= \frac{D_{t-1}}{D_t}$$

(3.4)

Theories of the yield curve

As we can observe by analysing yield curves in different markets at any time, a yield curve can be one of four basic shapes, which are:

- *normal:* in which yields are at "average" levels and the curve slopes gently upwards as maturity increases;
- *upward sloping (or positive or rising):* in which yields are at historically low levels, with long rates substantially greater than short rates;
- *downward sloping (or inverted or negative):* in which yield levels are very high by historical standards, but long-term yields are significantly lower than short rates;
- *humped:* where yields are high with the curve rising to a peak in the medium-term maturity area, and then sloping downwards at longer maturities.

Various explanations have been put forward to explain the shape of the yield curve at any one time, which we can now consider.

UNBIASED OR PURE EXPECTATIONS HYPOTHESIS

If short-term interest rates are expected to rise, then longer-dated yields should be higher than shorter ones to reflect this. If this were not the case, investors would only buy the shorter-dated bonds and roll over the investment when they matured. Likewise if rates are expected to fall then longer yields should be lower than short yields. The *expectations hypothesis* states that the long-term interest rate is a geometric average of expected future short-term rates. This was in fact the theory that was used to derive the forward yield curve in 3.2 and 3.3 previously. This gives us:

$$(1+rs_T)^T = (1+rs_1)(1+{}_1rf_2) \ldots (1+{}_Trf_T)$$

(3.5)

or

$$(1+rs_T)^T = (1+rs_{T-1})^{T-1}(1+{}_{T-1}rf_T)$$

(3.6)

where rs_T is the spot yield on a T-year bond and ${}_{t-1}rf_t$ is the implied one-year rate t years ahead. For example if the current one-year rate is $rs_1 = 6.5\%$ and the market is expecting the one-year rate in a year's time to be ${}_1rf_2 = 7.5\%$, then the market is expecting a £100 investment in two one-year bonds to yield:

£100 (1.065)(1.075) = £114.49

after two years. To be equivalent to this an investment in a two-year bond has to yield the same amount, implying that the current two-year rate is $rs_2 = 7\%$, as shown below.

£100 $(1.07)^2$ = £114.49

This result must be so, to ensure no arbitrage opportunities exist in the market and in fact we showed as much, earlier in the chapter when we considered forward rates.

A rising yield curve is therefore explained by investors expecting short-term interest rates to rise, that is ${}_1rf_2 > rs_2$. A falling yield curve is explained by investors expecting short-term rates to be lower in the future. A humped yield curve is explained by investors expecting short-term interest rates to rise and long-term rates to fall. Expectations, or views on the future direction of the market, are a function of the expected rate of inflation. If the market expects inflationary pressures in the future, the yield curve will be positively shaped, while if inflation expectations are inclined towards disinflation, then the yield curve will be negative.

LIQUIDITY PREFERENCE THEORY

Intuitively we can see that longer maturity investments are more risky than shorter ones. An investor lending money for a five-year term will usually demand a higher rate of interest than if he were to lend the same customer money for a five-week term. This is because the borrower may not be able to repay the loan over the longer time period as he may for instance, have gone bankrupt in that period. For this reason longer-dated yields should be higher than short-dated yields.

We can consider this theory in terms of inflation expectations as well. Where inflation is expected to remain roughly stable over time, the market would anticipate a positive yield curve. However the expectations hypothesis cannot by itself explain this phenomenon, as under stable inflationary conditions one would expect a flat yield curve. The risk inherent in longer-dated investments, or the *liquidity preference theory*, seeks to explain a positive shaped curve. Generally borrowers prefer to borrow over as long a term as possible, while lenders will wish to lend over as short a term as possible. Therefore, as we first stated, lenders have to be compensated for lending over the longer term; this compensation is considered a premium for a loss in *liquidity* for the lender. The premium is increased the further the investor lends across the term structure, so that the longest-dated investments will, all else being equal, have the highest yield.

SEGMENTATION HYPOTHESIS

The capital markets are made up of a wide variety of users, each with different requirements. Certain classes of investors will prefer dealing at the short-end of the yield curve, while others will concentrate on the longer end of the market. The *segmented markets* theory suggests that activity is concentrated in certain specific areas of the market, and that there are no inter-relationships between these parts of the market; the relative amounts of funds invested in each of the maturity spectrum causes differentials in supply and demand, which results in humps in the yield curve. That is, the shape of the yield curve is determined by supply and demand for certain specific maturity investments, each of which has no reference to any other part of the curve.

For example banks and building societies concentrate a large part of their activity at the short end of the curve, as part of daily cash management (known as *asset and liability management*) and for regulatory purposes (known as *liquidity requirements*). Fund managers such as pension funds and insurance companies however are active at the long end of the market. Few institutional investors however have any preference for medium-dated bonds. This behaviour on the part of investors will lead to high prices (low yields) at both the short and long ends of the yield curve and lower prices (higher yields) in the middle of the term structure.

FURTHER VIEWS ON THE YIELD CURVE

As one might expect there are other factors that affect the shape of the yield curve. For instance short-term interest rates are greatly influenced by the availability of funds in the money market. The slope of the yield curve (usually defined as the 10-year yield minus the three-month interest rates) is also a measure of the degree of tightness of government monetary policy. A low, upward sloping curve is often thought to be a sign that an environment of cheap money, due to a more loose monetary policy, is to be followed by a period of higher inflation and higher bond yields. Equally a high downward sloping curve is taken to mean that a situation of tight credit, due to more strict monetary policy, will result in falling inflation and lower bond yields.

Inverted yield curves have often preceded recessions; for instance '*The Economist*' in an article from April 1998 remarked that in the United States every recession since 1955 bar one has been preceded by a negative yield curve. The analysis is the same: if investors expect a recession they also expect inflation to fall, so the yields on long-term bonds will fall relative to short-term bonds. In the UK over the last two years, the explanation behind the inverted shape of the gilt yield curve has focused on two other factors: first, the handing of responsibility for setting interest rates to the *Monetary Policy Committee* (MPC) of the Bank of England, and secondly the expectation that the UK will abandon sterling and join the euro currency. The yield curve suggests that the market expects the MPC to be successful and keep inflation at a level around 2.5% over the long term (its target is actually a 1% range either side of 2.5%), and also that sterling interest rates will need to come down over the medium term as part of *convergence* with the conditions in euroland.

There is therefore significant information content in the yield curve, and economists and bond analysts will consider the shape of the curve as part of their policy making and investment advice. The shape of parts of the curve, whether the short-end or long-end, as well that of the entire curve, can serve as useful predictors of future market conditions. As part of an analysis it is also worthwhile considering the yield curves across several different markets and currencies. For instance the interest-rate swap curve, and its position relative to that of the government bond yield curve, is also regularly analysed for its information content. In developed country economies the interest-rate swap market is usually as liquid as the government bond market, if not more liquid, and so it is common to see the swap curve analysed when making predictions about say, the future level of short-term interest rates.

Government policy will influence the shape and level of the yield curve, including policy on public sector borrowing, debt management and open-market operations. The markets perception of the size of public sector debt will influence bond yields; for instance an increase in the level of debt can lead to an increase in bond yields across the maturity range. Open-market operations, which refers to the daily operation by the Bank of England to control the level of the money supply (to which end the Bank purchases short-term bills and also engages in repo dealing), can have a number of effects. In the short-term it can tilt the yield curve both upwards and downwards; longer term, changes in the level of the base rate will affect yield levels. An anticipated rise in base rates can lead to a drop in prices for short-term bonds, whose yields will be expected to rise; this can lead to a temporary inverted curve. Finally debt management policy will influence the yield curve. (In the United Kingdom this is now the responsibility of the Debt Management Office.) Much government debt is rolled over as it matures, but the maturity of the replacement debt can have a significant influence on the yield curve in the form of humps in the market segment in which the debt is placed, if the debt is priced by the market at a relatively low price and hence high yield.

Spot and Forward Rates: Boot-Strapping From The Par Yield Curve

SPOT RATES AND BOOT-STRAPPING

Par, spot and forward rates have a close mathematical relationship. Here we explain and derive these different interest rates and explain their application in the markets. Note that *spot* interest rates are also called zero-coupon rates, because they are the interest rates that would be applicable to a zero-coupon bond. The two terms are used synonymously, however strictly speaking they are not exactly similar. Zero-coupon bonds are actual market instruments, and the yield on zero-coupon bonds can be observed in the market. A spot rate is a purely theoretical construct, and so cannot actually be observed directly. For our purposes though, we will use the terms synonymously.

A *par* yield is the yield-to-maturity on a bond that is trading at par. This means that the yield is equal to the bond's coupon level. A zero-coupon bond is a bond which has no coupons, and therefore only one cash flow, the redemption payment on maturity. It is therefore a *discount* instrument, as it is issued at a discount to par and redeemed at par. The yield on a zero-coupon bond can be viewed as a true yield, at the time that is it purchased, if the paper is held to maturity. This is because no reinvestment of coupons is involved and so there are no interim cash flows vulnerable to a change in interest rates. Zero-coupon yields are the key determinant of value in the capital markets, and they are calculated and quoted for every major currency. Zero-coupon rates can be used to value any cash flow that occurs at a future date.

Where zero-coupon bonds are traded the yield on a zero-coupon bond of a particular maturity is the zero-coupon rate for that maturity. Not all debt capital trading environments possess a liquid market in zero-coupon bonds. However it is not necessary to have zero-coupon bonds in order to calculate zero-coupon rates. It is possible to calculate zero-coupon rates from a range of market rates and prices, including coupon bond yields, interest-rate futures and currency deposits.

We illustrate shortly the close mathematical relationship between par, zero-coupon and forward rates. We also illustrate how the boot-strapping technique could be used to calculate spot and forward rates from bond redemption yields. In addition, once the discount factors are known, any of these rates can be calculated. The relationship between the three rates allows the markets to price interest-rate swap and FRA rates, as a swap rate is the weighted arithmetic average of forward rates for the term in question.

DISCOUNT FACTORS AND THE DISCOUNT FUNCTION

It is possible to determine a set of *discount factors* from market interest rates. A discount factor is a number in the range zero to one which can be used to obtain the present value of some future value. We have:

$$PV_t = d_t \times FV_t$$

(3.7)

where

PV_t	is the present value of the future cash flow occurring at time t
FV_t	is the future cash flow occurring at time t
d_t	is the discount factor for cash flows occurring at time t

Discount factors can be calculated most easily from zero-coupon rates; equations 3.8 and 3.9 apply to zero-coupon rates for periods up to one year and over one year respectively.

$$d_t = \frac{1}{(1 + rs_t T_t)}$$

(3.8)

$$d_t = \frac{1}{(1 + rs_t)^{T_t}}$$

(3.9)

where

d_t	is the discount factor for cash flows occurring at time t
rs_t	is the zero-coupon rate for the period to time t
T_t	is the time from the value date to time t, expressed in years and fractions of a year

Individual zero-coupon rates allow discount factors to be calculated at specific points along the maturity term structure. As cash flows may occur at any time in the future, and not necessarily at convenient times like in three months or one year, discount factors often need to be calculated for every possible date in the future. The complete set of discount factors is called the *discount function*.

Implied Spot and Forward Rates [2]

In this section we describe how to obtain zero-coupon and forward interest rates from the yields available from coupon bonds, using a method known as *boot-strapping*. In a government bond market such as that for US Treasuries or UK gilts, the bonds are considered to be *default-free*. The rates from a government bond yield curve describe the risk-free rates of return available in the market *today*, however they also *imply* (risk-free) rates of return for *future time periods*. These implied future rates, known as *implied forward rates*, or simply *forward rates*, can be derived from a given spot yield curve using boot-strapping. This term reflects the fact that each calculated spot rate is used to determine the next period spot rate, in successive steps.

Table 3.1 shows an hypothetical benchmark gilt yield curve for value as at 7 December 2000. The observed yields of the benchmark bonds that compose the curve are displayed in the last column. All rates are annualised and assume semi-annual compounding. The bonds all pay on the same coupon dates of 7 June and 7 December, and as the value date is a coupon date, there is no accrued interest

[2] This section follows the approach described in Windas (1993), which provides an excellent introduction to boostrapping and spot and forward interest rates.

on any of the bonds.[3] The *clean* and *dirty* prices for each bond are identical.

Bond	Term to maturity (years)	Coupon	Maturity date	Price	Gross Redemption Yield
4% Treasury 2001	0.5	4%	07-Jun-01	100	4%
5% Treasury 2001	1	5%	07-Dec-01	100	5%
6% Treasury 2002	1.5	6%	07-Jun-02	100	6%
7% Treasury 2002	2	7%	07-Dec-02	100	7%
8% Treasury 2003	2.5	8%	07-Jun-03	100	8%
9% Treasury 2003	3	9%	07-Dec-03	100	9%

Table 3.1 Hypothetical UK government bond yields as at 7 December 2000

The gross redemption yield or *yield-to-maturity* of a coupon bond describes the single rate that present-values the sum of all its future cash flows to its current price. It is essentially the *internal rate of return* of the set of cash flows that make up the bond. This yield measure suffers from a fundamental weakness in that each cash-flow is present-valued at the same rate, an unrealistic assumption in anything other than a flat yield curve environment. So the yield to maturity is an *anticipated* measure of the return that can be expected from holding the bond from purchase until maturity. In practice it will only be achieved under the following conditions:

- the bond is purchased on issue;
- all the coupons paid throughout the bond's life are re-invested at the same yield to maturity at which the bond was purchased;
- the bond is held until maturity.

[3] Benchmark gilts pay coupon on a semi-annual basis on 7 June and 7 December each year.

In practice these conditions will not be fulfilled, and so the yield to maturity of a bond is not a true interest rate for that bond's maturity period.

The bonds in Table 3.1 pay semi-annual coupons on 7 June and 7 December and have the same time period - six months - between 7 December 2000, their valuation date and 7 June 2001, their next coupon date. However since each issue carries a different yield, the next six-month coupon payment for each bond is present-valued at a different rate. In other words, the six-month bond present-values its six-month coupon payment at its 4% yield to maturity, the one-year at 5%, and so on. Because each of these issues uses a different rate to present-value a cash flow occurring at the same future point in time, it is unclear which of the rates should be regarded as the true interest rate or benchmark rate for the six-month period from 7 December 2000 to 7 June 2001. This problem is repeated for all other maturities.

For the purposes of valuation and analysis however, we require a set of true interest rates, and so these must be derived from the redemption yields that we can observe from the benchmark bonds trading in the market. These rates we designate as rs_i, where rs_i is the *implied spot rate* or *zero-coupon rate* for the term beginning on 7 December 2000 and ending at the end of period i.

We begin calculating implied spot rates by noting that the six-month bond contains only one future cash flow, the final coupon payment and the redemption payment on maturity. This means that it is in effect trading as a zero-coupon bond, as there is only one cash flow left for this bond, is final payment. Since this cash flow's present value, future value and maturity term are known, the unique interest rate that relates these quantities can be solved using the compound interest equation (3.10) below.

$$FV = PV \times \left(1 + \frac{rs_i}{m}\right)^{(nm)}$$

$$rs_i = m \times \left(\sqrt[(nm)]{\frac{FV}{PV}} - 1\right)$$

(3.10)

where

FV	is the future value
PV	is the present value
rs_i	is the implied i-period spot rate
m	is the number of interest periods per year
n	is the number of years in the term

The first rate to be solved is referred to as the implied six-month spot rate and is the true interest rate for the six-month term beginning on 2 January and ending on 2 July 2000.

Equation 3.10 relates a cash flow's present value and future value in terms of an associated interest rate, compounding convention and time period. Of course if we re-arrange it, we may use it to solve for an implied spot rate. For the six-month bond the final cash flow on maturity is £102, comprised of the £2 coupon payment and the £100 (*par*) redemption amount. So we have for the first term, $i = 1$, FV = £102, PV = £100, n = 0.5 years and m = 2. This allows us to calculate the spot rate as follows:

$$rs_i = m \times \left(\sqrt[(nm)]{FV/PV} - 1\right)$$
$$rs_1 = 2 \times \left(\sqrt[(0.5 \times 2)]{£102/£100} - 1\right)$$
$$rs_1 = 0.04000$$
$$rs_1 = 4.000\%$$

(3.11)

Thus the implied six-month spot rate or zero-coupon rate is equal to 4 per cent.[4] We now need to determine the implied one-year spot rate for the term from 7 December 2000 to 7 June 2001. We note that the one-year issue has a 5% coupon and contains two future cash flows: a £2.50 six-month coupon payment on 7 June 2001 and a £102.50 one-year coupon and principal payment on 7 December 2001. Since the first cash flow occurs on 7 June - six months from now - it must be present-valued at the 4 per cent six-month spot rate established above. Once this present value is determined, it may be subtracted from the £100 total present value (its current price) of the one-year issue to obtain the present value of the one-year coupon and cash flow. Again we then have a single cash flow with a known present value, future value and term. The rate that equates these quantities is the implied one-year spot rate. From equation 3.10 the present value of the six-month £2.50 coupon payment of the one-year benchmark bond, discounted at the implied six-month spot rate, is:

$$PV_{\text{6-mo cash flow, 1-yr bond}} = £2.50/(1 + 0.04/2)^{(0.5 \times 2)}$$
$$= £2.45098$$

[4] Of course intuitively we could have concluded that the six-month spot rate was 4 per cent, without the need to apply the arithmetic, as we had already assumed that the six-month bond was a quasi-zero-coupon bond.

The present value of the one-year £102.50 coupon and principal payment is found by subtracting the present value of the six-month cash flow, determined above, from the total present value (current price) of the issue:

$$PV_{\text{1-yr cash flow, 1-yr bond}} = £100 - £2.45098$$
$$= £97.54902$$

The implied one-year spot rate is then determined by using the £97.54902 present value of the one-year cash flow determined above:

$$rs_2 = 2 \times \left(\sqrt[(1x2)]{£102.50/£97.54902} - 1 \right)$$
$$= 0.0501256$$
$$= 5.01256\%$$

The implied 1.5 year spot rate is solved in the same way:

$$PV_{\text{6-mo cash flow, 1.5-yr bond}} = £3.00 / (1 + 0.04 / 2)^{(0.5x2)}$$
$$= £2.94118$$

$$PV_{\text{1-yr cash flow, 1.5-yr bond}} = £3.00 / (1 + 0.0501256 / 2)^{(1x2)}$$
$$= £2.85509$$

$$PV_{\text{1.5-yr cash flow, 1.5-yr bond}} = £100 - £2.94118 - £2.85509$$
$$= £94.20373$$

$$
\begin{aligned}
rs_3 &= 2 \times \left(\sqrt[(1.5 \times 2)]{£103 / £94.20373} - 1\right) \\
&= 0.0604071 \\
&= 6.04071\%
\end{aligned}
$$

Extending the same process for the two-year bond, we calculate the implied two-year spot rate rs_4 to be 7.0906 per cent. The implied 2.5-year and three-year spot rates rs_5 and rs_6 are 8.1709 per cent 9.2879 per cent respectively.

The interest rates rs_1, rs_2, rs_3, rs_4, rs_5 and rs_6 describe the true zero-coupon interest rates for the six-month, one-year, 1.5-year, two-year, 2.5-year and three-year terms that begin on 7 December 2000 and end on 7 June 2001, 7 December 2001, 7 June 2002, 7 December 2002, 7 June 2003 and 7 December 2003 respectively. They are also called *implied spot rates* because they have been calculated from redemption yields observed in the market from the benchmark government bonds that were listed in Table 3.1.

Note that the one-, 1.5-, two-year, 2.5-year and three-year implied spot rates are progressively greater than the corresponding redemption yields for these terms. This is an important result, and occurs whenever the yield curve is positively sloped. The reason for this is that the present values of a bond's shorter-dated cash flows are discounted at rates that are lower than the bond's redemption yield; this generates higher present values that, when subtracted from the current price of the bond, produce a lower present value for the final cash flow. This lower present value implies a spot rate that is greater than the issue's yield. In an inverted yield curve environment we observe the opposite result, that is implied rates that lie below the corresponding redemption yields. If the redemption yield curve is flat, the implied spot rates will be equal to the corresponding redemption yields.

Once we have calculated the spot or zero-coupon rates for the six-month, one-year, 1.5-year, two-year, 2.5-year and three-year terms, we can determine the rate of return that is implied by the yield curve for the sequence of six-month periods beginning on 7 December 2000, 7 June 2001, 7 December 2001, 7 June 2002 and 7 December 2002. These period rates are referred to as *implied forward rates* or *forward-forward rates* and we denote these as rf_i , where rf_i is the implied six-month forward interest rate today for the ith period.

Since the implied six-month zero-coupon rate (spot rate) describes the return for a term that coincides precisely with the first of the series of six-month periods, this rate describes the risk-free rate of return for the first six-month period. It is therefore equal to the first period spot rate. Thus we have $rf_1 = rs_1 =$ 4.0 per cent, where rf_1 is the risk-free forward rate for the first six-month period beginning at period 1. We show now how the risk-free rates for the second, third, fourth, fifth and sixth six-month periods, designated rf_2, rf_3, rf_4, rf_5 and rf_6 respectively may be solved from the implied spot rates.

The benchmark rate for the second semi-annual period rf_2 is referred to as the one-period forward six-month rate, because it goes into effect one six-month period from now ("one-period forward") and remains in effect for six months ("six-month rate"). It is therefore the six-month rate in six months time, and is also referred to as the 6-month forward-forward rate. This rate, in conjunction with the rate from the first period rf_1, must provide returns that match those generated by the implied one-year spot rate for the entire one-year term. In other words, one pound invested for six months from 7 December 2000 to 7 June 2001 at the first period's benchmark rate of 4 per cent and then reinvested for another six months from 7 June 2001 to 7 December 2001 at the second period's (as yet unknown) implied *forward* rate must enjoy the same returns as one pound invested for one year from 7 December 2000 to 7 December 2001 at the implied one-year *spot* rate of 5.0125 per cent. This reflects the law of no-arbitrage.

A moment's thought will convince us that this must be so. If this were not the case, we might observe an interest rate environment in which the return received by an investor over any given term would depend on whether an investment is made at the start period for the entire maturity term or over a succession of periods within the whole term and re-invested. If there were any discrepancies between the returns received from each approach, there would exist an unrealistic arbitrage opportunity, in which investments for a given term carrying a lower return might be sold short against the simultaneous purchase of investments for the same period carrying a higher return, thereby locking in a risk-free, cost-free profit. Therefore forward interest rates must be calculated so that they are *arbitrage-free*. Forward rates are not therefore a prediction of what spot interest rates are likely to be in the future, rather a mathematically derived set of interest rates that reflect the current spot term structure and the rules of no-arbitrage. Excellent mathematical explanations of the no-arbitrage property of interest-rate markets are contained in Ingersoll (1987), Jarrow (1996), and Robert Shiller (1990) among others.

The existence of a no-arbitrage market of course makes it straightforward to calculate forward rates; we know that the return from an investment made over a period must equal the return made from investing in a shorter period and successively reinvesting to a matching term. If we know the return over the shorter period, we are left with only one unknown, the full-period forward rate, which is then easily calculated. In our example, having established the rate for the first six-month period, the rate for the second six-month period – the one-period forward six-month rate – is determined below.

The future value of £1 invested at rf_1, the period 1 forward rate, at the end of the first six-month period is calculated as follows:

$$\begin{aligned}
FV_1 &= £1 \times \left(1 + \frac{rf_1}{2}\right)^{(0.5 \times 2)} \\
&= £1 \times \left(1 + \frac{0.04}{2}\right)^1 \\
&= £1.02000
\end{aligned}$$

The future value of £1 at the end of the one-year term, invested at the implied benchmark one-year spot rate is determined as follows:

$$\begin{aligned}
FV_2 &= £1 \times \left(1 + \frac{rs_2}{2}\right)^{(1x2)} \\
&= £1 \times \left(1 + \frac{0.0501256}{2}\right)^2 \\
&= £1.050754
\end{aligned}$$

The implied benchmark one-period forward rate rf_2 is the rate that equates the value of FV_1 (£1.02) on 7 June 2001 to FV_2 (£1.050754) on 7 December 2001. From equation (3.x4) we have:

$$rf_2 = 2 \times \left(\sqrt[(0.5 \times 2)]{\frac{FV_2}{FV_1}} - 1 \right)$$

$$= 2 \times \left(\frac{£1.050754}{£1.02} - 1 \right)$$

$$= 0.060302$$

$$= 6.0302\%$$

In other words £1 invested from 7 December to 7 June at 4.0 per cent (the implied forward rate for the first period) and then reinvested from 7 June to 7 December 2001 at 6.0302 per cent (the implied forward rate for the second period) would accumulate the same returns as £1 invested from 7 December 2000 to 7 December 2001 at 5.01256 per cent (the implied one-year spot rate).

The rate for the third six-month period – the two-period forward six-month interest rate – may be calculated in the same way:

$$FV_2 = £1.050754$$

$$FV_3 = £1 \times (1 + rs3/2)^{(1.5 \times 2)}$$

$$= £1 \times (1 + 0.0604071/2)^3$$

$$= £1.093375$$

$$rf_3 = 2 \times \left(\sqrt[(0.5\times 2)]{\frac{FV_3}{FV_4}} - 1 \right)$$

$$= 2 \times \left(\sqrt[1]{£1.093375 / £1.050754} - 1 \right)$$

$$= 0.081125$$

$$= 8.1125\%$$

In the same way the three-period forward six-month rate rf_4 is calculated to be 10.27247 per cent. The rest of the results are shown in Table 3.2. We say *one-period* forward rate because it is the forward rate that applies to the six-month period. The results of the implied spot (zero-coupon) and forward rate calculations along with the given redemption yield curve are illustrated graphically in Figure 3.2.

The simple bootstrapping methodology can be applied using a spreadsheet for actual market redemption yields. However in practice we will not have a set of bonds with exact and/or equal periods to maturity and coupons falling on the same date. Nor will they all be priced conveniently at par. In designing a spreadsheet spot rate calculator therefore, the coupon rate and maturity date is entered as standing data and usually interpolation is used when calculating the spot rates for bonds with uneven maturity dates. A spot curve model that uses this approach in conjunction with the boot-strapping method is available for downloading at www.mchoudhry.co.uk. Market practitioners usually use discount factors to extract spot and forward rates from market prices. For an account of this method, see Choudhry *et al* (2001), Chapter 9.

Term to maturity	Yield to maturity	Implied spot rate	Implied one-period forward rate
0.5	4.0000%	4.00000%	4.00000%
1	5.0000%	5.01256%	6.03023%
1.5	6.0000%	6.04071%	8.11251%
2	7.0000%	7.09062%	10.27247%
2.5	8.0000%	8.17090%	12.24833%
3	9.0000%	9.28792%	14.55654%

Table 3.2 Implied spot and forward rates

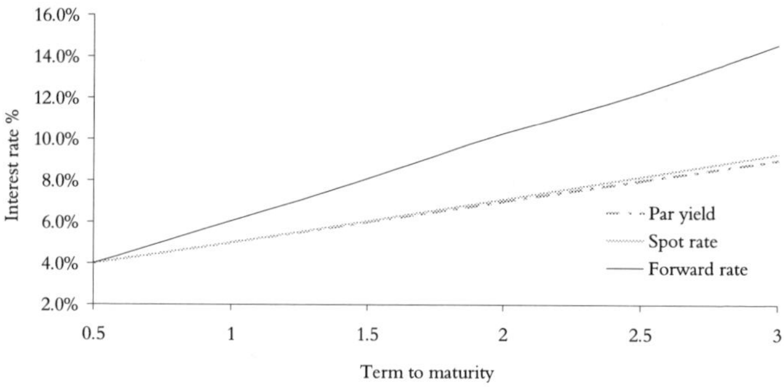

Figure 3.2 Par, spot and forward yield curves

REFERENCES

Choudhry, M., D. Joannas, R. Pereira, R. Pienaar, *Capital Markets Instruments: Analysis and Valuation*, FT Prentice Hall 2001

Ingersoll, J., *Theory of Financial Decision Making*, Bowman & Littlefield 1987, Chapter 18

Jarrow, R., *Modelling Fixed Income Securities and Interest Rate Options*, McGraw-Hill 1996, Chapters 2-3

Shiller, R., "The Term Structure of Interest Rates", in Friedman and Hahn (editors), *Handbook of Monetary Economics*, North-Holland 1990, Chapter 13

Windas T., *An Introduction to Option-Adjusted Spread Analysis*, Bloomberg Publications 1993, Chapter 3

Chapter 4

DURATION AND CONVEXITY

The previous chapters discussed the various methods used to calculate the returns from holding bonds. This chapter will look at the main method used to measure the *risk* exposure inherent in holding bonds. The risk under consideration here is *interest rate risk*; there are of course other risks in holding a bond. However the main risk in holding UK gilts will be interest rate risk, since gilts do not expose investors to any type of *credit risk*. Our analysis of yield curve shapes referred to the market's view of inflation. Inflation risk is common to all bonds, and the required return on bonds will reflect an inflation expectation element. Interest rate risk is also common to all bonds, and has an important effect on bond values. It is the risk that bond prices will fall if market interest rates rise, and is the main form of *market risk* for bonds and strips. The main measures of interest rate risk are *duration, modified duration* and *convexity*.

Duration

When analysing the properties of a bond, we would soon conclude that its maturity gives us little indication of the timing or size of its cash flows, and hence its sensitivity to moves in market interest rates. For example, if comparing two bonds with the same maturity date but different coupons, the higher coupon bond provides a larger proportion of its return in the form of coupon income than does the lower coupon bond. The higher coupon bond provides its return at a faster rate; its value is theoretically therefore less subject to subsequent fluctuations in interest rates. We can measure the speed of payment of a bond, and hence its price risk relative to other bonds of the same maturity by measuring the average maturity of the bond's cash flow stream. Bond analysts use *duration* to measure this property (it is also known as *Macaulay's duration*, after its inventor, who first introduced it in 1938). Duration is the weighted average time until the receipt of cash flows from a bond, where the weights are the present values of the cash flows, measured in years.

We can illustrate a simple duration calculation, using an example of a 5–year bond with precisely five years to maturity and a coupon of 8 per cent. Assume that the bond is priced at par, giving a yield to maturity of 8 per cent. The bond's cash flows are shown in Table 4.1, along with a diagram of the timing of cash flows.

Cash Flow	Present Value	Timing (T)	PV × T
8	7.41	1	7.41
8	6.86	2	13.72
8	6.35	3	19.05
8	5.88	4	23.52
108	73.50	5	367.51
	100.00		**431.25**

Table 4.1

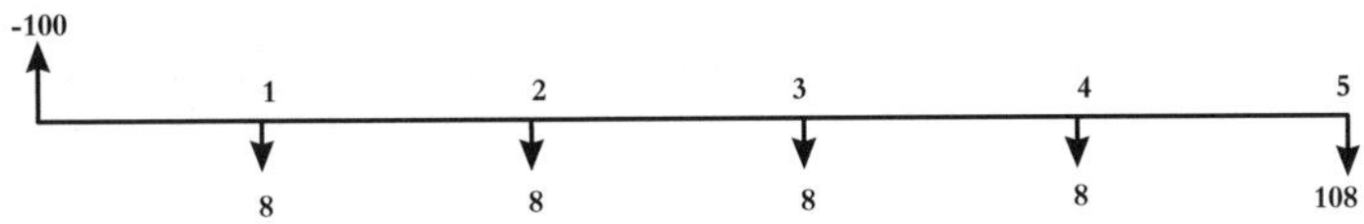

Fig 4.1 Receipt of cash flows for 8% 5–year bond (time line)

The present value is calculated in the normal way, hence for period 2 the present value is $[8/(1.08)^2]$, which gives us 6.859. Duration is calculated as 431.21 / 100, which is equal to 4.31 years. This implies that the average time taken to receive the cash flows on this bond is 4.31 years. This is shown in figure 4.2 in our "duration fulcrum", with 4.31 years being the time to the pivot, marked from A to B. The coupons are shown as "C", and these diminish progressively as their present value decreases.

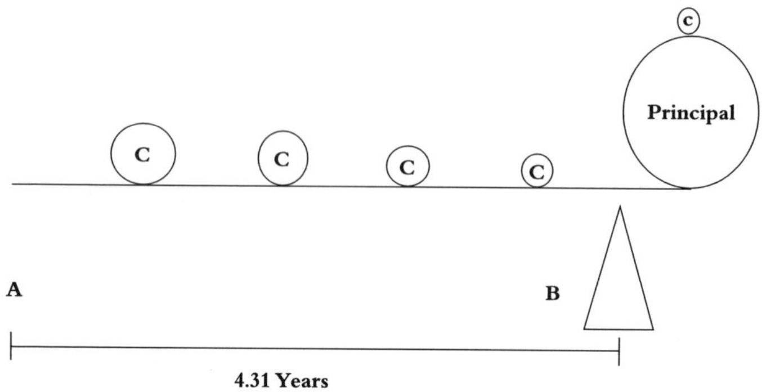

Fig 4.2 The Duration Fulcrum

We can illustrate the duration calculation mathematically as shown in equation 4.1.

$$D = \frac{C}{P_d} \sum_{t=1}^{T} \frac{t}{(1+r)^t} + \frac{M}{P_d} \frac{T}{(1+r)^T}$$

(4.1)

where

D is the duration measured in years
C is the annual coupon
M is the par value of the bond
P_d is the dirty price of the bond
t is the time in years to the tth cash flow
T is the time to maturity in years
r is the yield to maturity

In 4.1 as $d/(1+r)^t$ is the discounted value of the tth cash flow, $d/P_d\ (1+r)^t$ is the relative discounted value of the tth cash flow and also the redemption value. We can illustrate this with an example; consider a bond with an annual coupon of 5% and precisely three years to maturity, trading at par. This gives values of $P_d = M = 100$, $C = £10$, $r = 5\%$ and $T = 3$ years. The duration of this bond is therefore:

$$D = \frac{10}{100}\left[\frac{1}{(1.05)} + \frac{2}{(1.05)^2} + \frac{3}{(1.05)^3}\right] + \frac{100}{100}\left[\frac{3}{(1.05)^3}\right]$$

$$= 2.89$$

As in our earlier example this implies that the average time taken to receive the cash flows on this bond is 2.89 years.

Let us examine some of the properties of duration. A bond's duration is always less than its maturity. This is because some weight is given to the cash flows in the early years of the bond's life, which brings forward the average time at which cash flows are received. In our example of the three–year bond, the coupon element contributes 0.4 years to duration, while the principal element contributes 2.49 years. Duration also varies with coupon, yield and maturity. The following three factors imply higher duration for a bond:

- the lower the coupon;
- the lower the yield;
- broadly, the longer the maturity.

For a zero–coupon bond, duration is equal to the maturity. This can be seen from the definition of a zero–coupon bond (all of its cash flow is received on maturity) and also from 4.1 given that $C = 0$ and $P_d = M/(1+r)^T$.

For an irredeemable bond duration is given by:

$$D = \frac{1}{rc}$$

(4.2)

where $rc = (d/P_d)$ is the *running yield* (or *current yield*) of the bond. This follows from 4.1 as $T \rightarrow \infty$, recognising that for an irredeemable bond $r = rc$. Equation 4.2 provides the limiting value to duration. For bonds trading at or above par duration increases with maturity and approaches this limit from below. For bonds trading at a discount to par duration increases to a maximum at around 20 years and then declines towards the limit given by 4.2. So in general, duration increases with maturity.

Duration increases as coupon and yield decrease. As the coupon falls, more of the relative weight of the cash flows is transferred to the maturity date and this causes duration to rise. Because the coupon on index–linked gilts is much lower than on conventional gilts, this means that the duration of index–linked gilts will be much higher than for conventional gilts of the same maturity. As yield increases, the present values of all future cash flows fall, but the present values of the more distant cash flows fall relatively more than those of the nearer cash flows. This has the effect of increasing the relative weight given to nearer cash flows and hence of reducing duration.

We can now demonstrate how duration is a measure of interest rate risk. To recap from the earlier section on bond pricing and yields, the present value equation for an annual coupon bond is given by:

$$P_d = \sum_{t=1}^{T} \frac{C}{(1+r)^t} + \frac{M}{(1+r)^T}$$

(4.3)

Differentiating this equation with respect to $(1+r)$ results in:

$$\frac{\Delta P_d}{\Delta(1+r)} = -C\sum_{t=1}^{T} \frac{t}{(1+r)^{t+1}} - M\frac{T}{(1+r)^{T+1}}$$

(4.4)

Multiplying both sides of 4.4 by $(1+r)/P_d$ gives us:

$$\frac{\Delta P_d / P_d}{\Delta(1+r)/(1+r)} = -\frac{C}{P_d}\sum_{t=1}^{T} \frac{t}{(1+r)^t} - \frac{M}{P_d}\frac{T}{(1+r)^T}$$

$$= -D$$

(4.5)

The left–hand side of 4.5 is the elasticity of the bond price with respect to (one plus) the yield to maturity; the right–hand side is the negative of duration. So duration measures the interest rate elasticity of the bond price, and is therefore a measure of interest rate risk. The lower the duration, the less responsive is the bond's value to interest rate fluctuations.

Figure 4.3 shows the present value profile for a bond. There is a negative–sloping, convex relationship between the (natural logarithm of) the price of the bond and the (natural logarithm of) one plus the yield to maturity. The slope of the present value profile at the current bond price and yield to maturity is equal to the (negative of the) duration of the bond. The flatter the present value profile, the lower the duration and the lower the interest rate risk.

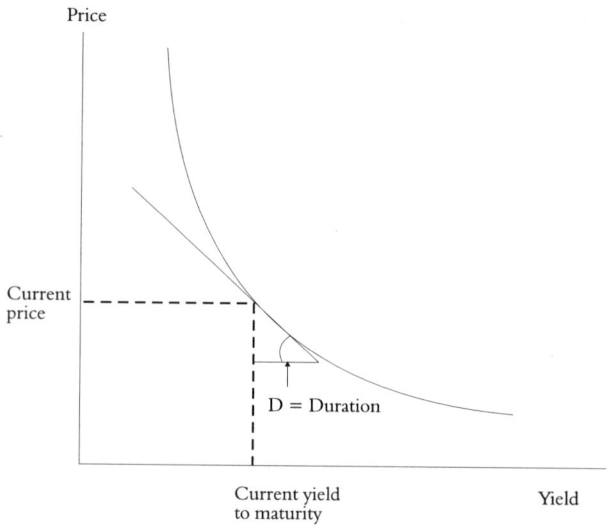

Fig 4.3 Present Value / Yield profile and duration

Modified Duration

From the Macaulay duration of a bond can be derived its *modified duration*, which gives a measure of the sensitivity of a bond's price to small changes in yield. The relationship between modified duration and duration is given by the following equation.

$$MD = \frac{D}{1+r}$$

(4.6)

where *MD* is the modified duration in years. For a gilt, which pays semi–annual coupons, the equation becomes:

$$MD = \frac{D}{\left(1 + \frac{r}{2}\right)}$$

(4.7)

This means that the following relationship holds between modified duration and bond prices:

$$\Delta P_d = MD \times \Delta r \times P_d$$

(4.8)

Example 4.1: Duration and modified duration

A 5 per cent annual coupon bond is trading at par with a duration of 2.85 years. If yields rise from 5% to 5.5%, then the price of the bond will fall by:

$$\Delta P_d = -D \times \frac{\Delta(r)}{1+r} \times P_d$$

$$= -(2.85) \times \left(\frac{0.005}{1.05}\right) \times 100$$

$$= -£1.357$$

That is, the price of the bond will now be £98.64.

The modified duration of a bond with a duration of 2.85 years and yield of 5% can be calculated to be

$$MD = \frac{2.85}{1.05}$$

which gives us *MD* equal to 2.71 years.

In the earlier example of the five-year bond with a duration of 4.31 years, the modified duration can be calculated to be 3.99. This tells us that for a 1 per cent move in the yield to maturity, the price of the bond will move (in the opposite direction) by 3.99%.

We can use modified duration to approximate bond prices for a given yield change. This is illustrated with the following expression:

$$\Delta P_d = -MD \times (\Delta r) \times P_d$$

For a bond with a modified duration of 3.24, priced at par, an increase in yield of 1 basis point (100 basis = 1 per cent) leads to a fall in the bond's price of:

$$\Delta P_d = (-3.24 / 100) \times (+0.01) \times 100.00$$

$$\Delta P_d = \text{£}0.0324, \text{ or } 3.24 \text{ pence}$$

In this case 3.24 pence is the *basis point value* of the bond, which is the change in the bond price given a 1 basis point change in the bond's yield. The basis point value of a bond can be calculated using:

$$BPV = \frac{MD}{100} \cdot \frac{P_d}{100}$$

Basis Point Value

This is also known as the *price value of a basis point* and as noted above is the change in the price of a bond if the yield changes by 1 basis point. This measure refers to cash price volatility as opposed to percentage price volatility, which is the price change as a percentage of the initial price. The price volatility is the same for an increase or a decrease of 1 basis point in yield, but for large changes in yield the price volatility will not be equal for movements of the same size but in different directions. To illustrate this we show in Table 4.2 the calculations for five hypothetical bonds and their relative basis point value.

Bond	Initial Price (8% yield)	Price at 8.01%	Basis Point Value*
5-year, 8% coupon	100.0000	99.9604	0.0396
25-year, 8% coupon	100.0000	99.9013	0.0987
5-year, 5% coupon	88.1309	88.0945	0.0364
5-year strip	64.3928	64.3620	0.0308
25-year strip	11.0710	11.0445	0.0265

* *absolute value per £100 of par value*

Table 4.2

Some market participants will also use *yield value of a price change* as a measure of bond price volatility. This indicates the change in yield of a bond for a specified change in price, measured in basis points.

The coupon and term to maturity of conventional bonds determine their price volatility. For a given term to maturity and initial yield, the price volatility of a bond is greater the lower the coupon rate. For a given coupon rate and initial yield, the longer the term to maturity the greater will be the price volatility. This tends to imply that bondholders who wish to increase a portfolio's price volatility because they expect interest rates to fall (and hence bond prices to rise) should hold long–dated bonds in the portfolio. If interest rates are expected to rise, investors should hold shorter–dated bonds.

Convexity

Duration can be regarded as a first–order measure of interest rate risk: it measures the *slope* of the present value/yield profile. It is however only an approximation of the actual change in bond price given a small change in yield to maturity. Similarly for modified duration, which describes the price sensitivity of a bond to small changes in yield. The approximation can break down under large changes in yield. This is because it is a straight line approximation of one point on a non–linear curve. This was shown in figure 4.3. The tangent drawn through at the point of measurement has a slope proportional to the bond's modified duration, which is calculated as:

$$-(MD) \times P_d$$

Convexity can be regarded as a second–order measure of interest rate risk; it measures the *curvature* of the present value/yield profile. Convexity can be regarded as an indication of the error we make when using duration and modified duration, as it measures the degree to which the curvature of a bond's price/yield relationship diverges from the straight–line estimation. The convexity of a bond is positively related to the dispersion of its cash flows thus, other things being equal, if one bond's cash flows are more spread out in time than another's, then it will have a higher *dispersion* and hence a higher convexity. Convexity is also positively related to duration.

The second–order differential of the present value equation 4.3 with respect to r is:

$$\frac{\Delta P_d}{P_d} = \frac{1}{P_d}\frac{\Delta P_d}{\Delta r}(\Delta r) + \frac{1}{2P_d}\frac{\Delta^2 P_d}{\Delta r^2}(\Delta r)^2$$

$$= -MD(\Delta r) + \frac{CV}{2}(\Delta r)^2$$

(4.9)

where

MD	is the modified duration
CV	is the convexity.

From 4.9 convexity is the rate at which price variation to yield changes with respect to yield. That is, it describes a bond's modified duration changes with respect to changes in interest rates. It can be approximated by expression 4.10.

$$CV = 10^8\left(\frac{\Delta P'_d}{P_d} + \frac{\Delta P''_d}{P_d}\right)$$

(4.10)

where

$\Delta P'_d$	is the change in bond price if yield increases by 1 basis point (0.01)
$\Delta P''_d$	is the change in bond price if yield decreases by 1 basis point (0.01)

It can be shown that convexity increases with the square of maturity. It decreases with both coupon and yield. Index–linked bonds are more convex than conventional bonds. The price/yield profile will be more convex for a bond of higher convexity; such a bond will outperform a bond of lower convexity whatever happens to market interest rates. High convexity is therefore a desirable property for bonds to have. In principle a more convex bond should fall in price less than a less convex one when yields rise, and rise in price more when yields fall. That is, convexity can be equated with the potential to outperform. Thus other things being equal, the higher the convexity of a bond the more desirable it should in principle be to investors. In some cases investors may be prepared to accept a bond with a lower yield in order to gain convexity. Convexity is in principle of more value if uncertainty, and hence expected market volatility, is high. Convexity is almost always positive. Negative convexity resulting from a bond with a concave price/yield profile would not be a benefit to a bondholder. The best example of bonds exhibiting negative convexity is when callable bonds approach the price at which they will be called.

When convexity is high, the duration measurement for interest rate risk becomes more inaccurate as changes in yield become large. In such situations it becomes necessary to use the approximation calculated by expression 4.9.

Interest rate risk for Strips

As we illustrated in the opening section of this chapter, strips have a longer duration than equivalent maturity conventional bonds. Their duration is equal in time to their maturity. The duration of a strip will decline roughly in parallel with time, whereas for a conventional bond the decline will be less. For a given modified duration, a strip will be less convex than a coupon bond. The following points highlight some of the salient points about how duration and convexity of strips compare with those of coupon bonds:

- strips have a Macaulay duration equal to their time in years to maturity;
- strips have a higher duration than coupon bonds of the same maturity;
- strips are *more* convex than coupon bonds of the same maturity;
- strips are less convex than coupon bonds of the same duration.

The reason that a strip is less convex than a conventional coupon bond of the same duration is that the coupon bond will have more dispersed cash flows than the strip. Although strips are less convex than bonds of identical duration, the highest duration conventional gilt (6% Treasury 2028) at March 1999 had a duration of 15.56 years (modified duration 15.26), whereas the principal strip from that bond had a duration of 29.77 years (modified duration 29.14). Long strips are therefore the most convex instruments in the gilt market.

Example 4.2: Switches and duration matched strategies

Consider a portfolio of £40 million in five–year bonds. The fund manager expects a rise shortly of 10 basis points in five–year bond yields. He has four possible strategies: he can do nothing, move into shorter– dated bonds, move into longer–dated bonds, or move into a combination of short– and long–dated bonds. The basis point values for various bonds are shown below.

Bond	**BPV**
3–year	0.022898
5–year	0.041583
10–year	0.059404

The fund manager decides to switch out of the five–year bond and into three–year bonds. In order to maintain his overall risk position, he has to calculate the nominal value of the new holding.

$$\frac{\text{BPV current position}}{\text{BPV proposed position}} = \frac{0.041583}{0.022898} = 1.816$$

Therefore his new holding will be £40m x 1.816 = £72.64 million of the three–year bond.

Parallel Shift

Assume that the yield curve shifted upwards by 10 basis points. We use the basis point values to calculate the loss on the position, as the price of the bonds has now fallen. The loss on the old position is:

$$\frac{0.041583}{100} \times 10 \times £40\text{m}$$

= £166,332

The loss on the new position would be:

$$\frac{0.022898}{100} \times 10 \times £72.68$$

= £166,332

Continued overleaf

We can see that the fund manager's risk position has not changed with respect to parallel shifts in the yield curve.

Butterfly / Barbell Spreads

The fund manager can combine a holding in both short–dated and long–dated bonds, against a short position in medium–dated bonds, resulting in a position that is also risk–neutral to parallel shifts in the yield curve. In this example the risk exposure in the short position must be balanced exactly by the risk exposure resulting from the two long positions.

Example 4.3

Consider a 10% sterling Eurobond maturing on 10 February 2009. For settlement on 10 February 1999 it was trading at 118.00 with a Macaulay duration of 7.46 years and a yield of 7.535%. Calculate:

(a) the modified duration

$$MD = \frac{\text{Macaulay duration}}{(1 + \text{yield})} = \frac{7.46}{1.07535}$$

$$= 6.937$$

(b) the basis point value

$$BPV = \frac{MD}{100} \times \frac{PV}{100} = \frac{6.937}{100} \times 1.18$$

$$= 0.0819$$

(c) What would the bond price be if its yield fell by 1 basis point?
As the yield has fallen by 1 basis point, the new price will be 118.08.

(d) If the bond price rises to 120.00, resulting in a yield of 7.294% and a Macaulay duration of 7.49 years, what is the bond's new basis point value?
The new modified duration is 7.49 / 1.07294, which is 6.981. Using the same formula again we calculate the new basis point value to be 0.0838.

Chapter 5

THE GILT STRIPS MARKET

The introduction of gilt strips was part of a range of measures developed by the Bank of England (BoE) and HM Treasury in connection with the modernisation and reform of the gilt market. These measures included changes in debt management strategy (now the responsibility of the *Debt Management Office* - DMO), issuance procedures, market infrastructure and the secondary market. The authorities also reviewed the types of gilt investment available to the market and to existing and potential investors. The most important development in this area was the introduction of gilt repo and gilt strips. An outline of the mechanics, trading and use of strips, together with notes on legal, regulatory and taxation issues, is contained in *The Official Gilt Strips Facility* published by the BoE in October 1997. This is a useful reference document and may be obtained free from the Bank.

Market Mechanics

INTRODUCTION

An official gilt stripping facility was first made possible by the tax reform announced by the Chancellor in July 1995. This paved the way for the payment of gross coupons. The BoE announced in November 1995 that the *Central Gilts Office* (CGO) system was to be upgraded to provide for the settlement of repo and strips; the upgraded system was introduced in November 1997. As we noted earlier, stripping is the process of separating a standard coupon bond into its individual coupon and principal payments, which are then separately held and traded in their own right as zero-coupon bonds. For example a ten-year gilt can be stripped into 21 zero-coupon bonds, comprised of one bond from the principal repayment and twenty from the semi-annual coupons. Coupon payments due in six, twelve, eighteen and so on months from the stripping date would become six, twelve, eighteen and so on month zero-coupon bonds. In an earlier section we explained how the prices of such bonds are related to the yield curve derived from conventional bonds, and considered the duration and convexity properties of strips. We also illustrated the general rule that if a yield curve is upward sloping (positive), the zero-coupon yield curve will lie above the conventional bond yield curve, while if the conventional curve is inverted, the zero-coupon curve will lie below it.

The introduction of the CGO upgrade allowed the gilt strips facility to be introduced on 8 December 1997. The market began quietly with relatively low volumes of trading. After one month's trading, under 1% of the (then) £82 billion of strippable stock was held in stripped form (BoE; *QB 2/98*). In this time turnover in the strips market, for both coupon and principal strips, amounted to 1% of turnover in the conventional gilt market (*ibid*).

Note that CGO merged with CREST in July 2000 and is now known as CREST-CGO or simply CREST.

Gilts held in CREST can be stripped or reconstituted by *gilt-edged market makers* (GEMMs). Strips are fully fledged gilts; they remain registered securities and liabilities of HM Government, therefore they have identical credit risk compared to conventional gilts. As they are registered securities, a BoE register is kept for a 7 June zero-coupon gilt issue and for a 7 December zero-coupon issue for each year up to and including 7 December 2028, the redemption date for the current longest-maturity gilt. Two strips will mature on that date, the coupon strip and principal date; the BoE keeps separate registers for coupon and principal strips.

PROPERTIES OF STRIPS

We have noted that strips are fully-fledged gilts, registered securities and liabilities of the government. They are stripped and reconstituted via the CREST facility, on the direction of GEMMs. It is not possible to remove a strip from CREST and hold it in paper form. Although any investor can hold and trade strips, they are not available via the National Savings Stock Register, the facility that allows private investors to buy and sell conventional gilts through the Post Office. Private investors must buy and sell gilts through a stockbroker. This was deemed necessary because the greater volatility of strip prices compared to conventional gilts was thought to make them unsuitable for certain types of personal investor; therefore the authorities did not want to make it possible for these investors to buy strips via the Post Office. Having to deal through a stockbroker should lead to private investors acquiring sufficient knowledge about the properties of strips.

Stripped coupons from different gilts but with the same coupon dates are fully fungible; this increases their liquidity. At the moment there is no fungibility between coupon and principal strips, although this remains under review and may be possible at a later date. All strippable gilts have the same coupon dates, 7 June and 7 December each year, so that all strips mature on these dates each year. A strippable gilt continues to trade as a conventional gilt; payments to holders of the unstripped bond are not affected. Where an issue is stripped, the remaining nominal amount of that bond trades as an unstripped gilt.

Strips are not deliverable into the LIFFE long-gilt futures contract; for this it is necessary to deliver a coupon gilt from amongst those in the delivery basket.

MECHANICS OF STRIPPING FACILITY

The minimum strippable amount for all gilts is £10,000 nominal. This can then be increased in units of £10,000 nominal. There is no limit on the amount or proportion of a strippable gilt issue that can be stripped or reconstituted. The CREST system includes a forward input facility for stripping and reconstitution requests to be entered up to one month in advance. GEMMs include strips trading as part of their general market making obligations.

STRIPPABLE GILTS

There are currently 46 gilts in issue, including floating rate, double-dated and irredeemable gilts but excluding index-linked gilts.

At table 5.1 is a list of strippable gilts and the amount held in stripped form as at 31 March 2000; for comparison we also show the amount of strips in issue as at 31 March 1998.

Stock	Redemption date	Amount in Issue (£mn)		Amount held in Stripped form (£mn)	
		31/03/00	31/03/98	31/03/00	31/03/98
8% Treasury 2000	07-Dec-00	9,800	9,800	88	314
7% Treasury 2002	07-Jun-02	9,000	9,000	206	198
6½% Treasury 2003	07-Dec-03	7,987	2,000	94	27
5% Treasury 2004	07-Jun-04	7,408	-	1	-
8½% Treasury 2005	07-Dec-05	10,373	10,373	465	304
7½% Treasury 2006	07-Dec-06	11,700	11,700	304	40
7¼% Treasury 2007	07-Dec-07	11,000	11,000	294	163
5¾% Treasury 2009	07-Dec-09	8,827	-	81	-
8% Treasury 2015	07-Dec-15	12,287	13,787	179	237
8% Treasury 2021	07-Jun-21	16,500	16,500	294	600
6% Treasury 2028	07-Dec-28	11,512	2,000*	294	-

** 6% Treasury 2028 eligible for stripping following auction on 20 May 1998, which took amount in issue to £5 billion, (Source: DMO)*

Table 5.1 List of Strippable Stocks and Amount Stripped. (Source: DMO)

The full list of strips as at March 1999, with their prices and yields, is given in Appendix I.

Table 5.1 shows that the amount of gilts held in stripped form stayed in the range of 1% to 4.5% of total nominal value during 2000. The BoE stated before the start of the strips market that all new benchmark issues would now be eligible for stripping. All strippable stocks have the same coupon dates (7 June and 7 December), which has allowed all coupon strips to be fungible. The BoE has left open the possibility of making coupon and principal strips fungible, and whether to introduce a second set of coupon dates.

There is no limit on the amount or proportion of any strippable gilt that can be stripped.

The BoE's view on fungibility of coupons and principal strips is that it would allow, in theory, the reconstituting of a greater amount of a coupon gilt. This would cause uncertainty for the holders of the coupon gilt, as its issue size would be uncertain. It is also not a feature of overseas strips markets. For related reasons, principal and principal strips are not fungible, even where redemption payments of two stocks fall on the same day. This situation may arise with for example, the principal strip of a five-year gilt issued five years after a ten-year gilt.

An extra set of coupon dates would increase investor choice over the timing of cash flows, however it may reduce liquidity in the market. For this reason it has not been introduced as yet but remains a possibility for the future.

PRICING CONVENTION

The BoE consulted with GEMMs before the introduction of the strips market on the preferred method for pricing strips. The result of this consultation was announced in May 1997 when the Bank stated that strips would trade on a yield basis rather than a price basis. The day count convention adopted, in both the conventional and strips market, was actual/actual; this was changed from the previous method of actual/365 on 1 November 1997. Those GEMMs who had preferred to quote strips on a price basis claimed that there may have been difficulties with agreeing a standard formula for converting yields into prices. A standard formula was therefore agreed.

After further consultation the following market standard formula was adopted for use in the market:

$$P = \frac{100}{\left(1 + \frac{r}{2}\right)^{\frac{d}{s}+n}}$$

(5.1)

where

P	is the price per £100 nominal of the strip
r	is the gross redemption yield (decimal)
d	is the exact number of days from the settlement date to the next quasi-coupon date
s	is exact number of days in the quasi-coupon period in which the settlement date falls
n	is the number of remaining quasi-coupon periods after the current period.

The r and s values are not adjusted for non-working days. A *quasi-coupon date* is a date on which a coupon would be due if the bond was a conventional coupon bond rather a strip. For example a strip maturing on 7 December 2005 would have quasi-coupon dates of 7 June and 7 December each year until maturity. A *quasi-coupon period* is defined to be the period between consecutive quasi-coupon dates. There are always six calendar months, regardless of the nature of the first coupon. For example a gilt settling on its issue date (assuming this is not also a quasi-coupon date) will have a quasi-coupon period which starts on the quasi-coupon date prior to the issue date and ends on the first quasi-coupon date following the issue date.

This method is also used in the US strips market, often referred to as the US "street" convention. The formula uses simple interest for the shortest strip, which is consistent with money market convention, and compound interest for all other strips which is then consistent with gilt market convention. The shortest strip is discounted on an actual/actual basis, which is inconsistent with sterling money market convention but is consistent with the convention followed in the gilt market. All other strips are discounted on an actual/actual basis. Using this method results in a jump in price when the shortest-but-one strip becomes the shortest since the formula switches from discounting on a compound interest basis to a simple interest basis.

For strips with only one quasi-coupon period remaining, equation 5.2 is used.

$$P = \frac{100}{\left(1 + \frac{d}{s} \cdot \frac{r}{2}\right)}$$

(5.2)

Yields are quoted to three decimal places; cash prices are calculated to six decimal places. The rounding convention is to round the third decimal place up by one if the fourth (or seventh) decimal place is 5 or above, and then to shorten at the third decimal place.

Stripping and reconstitution procedures

The BoE's paper "*The Official Gilt Strips Facility*" (October 1997) outlines in some detail the procedures involved in stripping and reconstituting. This section summarises the salient points from that document.

AVAILABILITY OF THE FUNCTIONALITY

Market participants who hold gilts within CREST, either in their own account or via an agent bank, are able to hold strips in CREST. Stripping itself can only be carried out at the direction of GEMMs (it can also be carried out by the BoE), so that non-GEMMs need to buy strips in the market or strip a gilt that they own via the services of a GEMM. Private investors must buy and sell strips via a stockbroker.

STRIPPING BY GEMMS

The information required from GEMMs when making a request to strip a gilt was outlined by the BoE prior to the start of trading in the market. This information includes the following:

- a unique transaction reference;
- the value date required (which can be up to a month in advance):
- the GEMMs CREST account number;
- the nominal amount of strips required;
- the unique reference number of the stock to be stripped, known as the "ISIN" number;
- the client identification number.

When a request is received it will be validated by the CREST system to ensure that the requesting party is eligible to strip stock, that the stock is strippable and that the quantity requested is in units acceptable by the system.

RECONSTITUTION BY GEMMS

On receipt of a request for reconstitution the system will deliver a coupon-bearing gilt in exchange for the relevant principal strip together with appropriate amounts of all coupon strips representing the gilt's cash flows that have not yet matured. The information that needs to be provided when making a reconstitution request is basically identical to that required when making a request to strip stock. Before reconstitution can occur the system will check that a sufficient amount of constituent strips are held in the requesting party's account. If there is an insufficient amount, the request is held in a "queue" until such sufficient amount becomes available.

MINIMUM UNITS FOR STRIPPING

Prior to the start of trading the BoE stated that for each strippable stock there would be a minimum amount below which the CGO system would not accept a request to strip stock. This procedure has been in place from the start. Such a ruling is required because nominal holdings of a gilt, whether an unstripped bond or a strip, must be in minimum multiples of £0.01. As the BoE states,

> "this implies that for example, at least £4 of a bond [is needed] to be stripped if the annual interest payable was say, 7½% because each six-month coupon would be denominated in ¼ percentage points (in this case a coupon of 3¾%). In the same way the minimum

> strippable amount of a $7^1/_4$% stock would need to be £8, and of a $7^1/_8$% stock £16."
> *(BoE, 1997 p.12)*

The system also requires minimum units for the strippability of stock in amounts above the minimum and for a minimum reconstitutable amount. Again using the Bank's example, for a $7^1/_4$% coupon gilt it is not possible to reconstitute an amount of say, £500 as the necessary coupon strips would be £18.125p and thus not in whole pence. The minimum strippable amount for gilts is £10,000 nominal, which can be increased in multiples of £10,000. This is the same minimum amount required in reconstituting a gilt. These minimum amounts can be varied and if this is deemed acceptable it will be announced at the time of issue of the gilt.

In secondary market trading strips can be transferred, exactly as with conventional gilts, in units of one penny nominal value.

Uses of Strips

ADVANTAGES OF ZERO-COUPON BONDS

Strips are a flexible new instrument in the sterling bond markets. They have a large number of uses for investors and traders. The following properties of strips make them attractive to market participants:

- simplicity of one cash flow at maturity allows matching to future liabilities;
- more precise management of cash flows;
- no reinvestment risk, as associated with conventional coupon-bearing bonds;
- holdings can be tailored to portfolio sensitivities;
- higher duration and convexity than conventional bonds of the same maturity, which would be useful for either duration weighting a portfolio or for taking risk positions;
- tax advantages in certain jurisdictions.

Strips are arguably the most basic cash flow structure available in the capital markets, being as they are zero-coupon paper. By investing in a portfolio of strips an investor is able to construct a desired pattern of cash flows, one that matches more precisely his investment requirements. In theory therefore there is a high demand for strips in the market. Domestic institutional investors with an interest at the long end of the yield curve will have a demand for long-dated strips, for example, life assurance companies and pension funds who have liabilities up to 30 years or more into the future. While strips can help to meet this demand, due to their providing a known amount at the end of a long-dated investment horizon, they are also attractive in that they present no reinvestment risk. The rate of return gained from buying a strip today and holding to maturity will be a true yield.

Retail investors and their advisers are also interested in strips because they allow them to have investments with cash flows of their choice. Where private investors wish to invest for a known future commitment they can also hold strips and realise the precise amount required.

We can summarise the main uses of strips as follows:

- matching long liabilities (pension funds);
- matching cash flows (insurance companies wishing to match their actuary-estimated payments, interested in acquiring forward-starting annuities);
- collateralisation of guarantees (financial companies, for example firms selling products with a guaranteed return, such as a guaranteed equity fund or minimum return stock-market linked TESSA/ISA or other account);
- expressing views on sterling interest rates (commercial and investment banks, foreign investors and money market funds);
- Taking advantage of the high duration of strips (hedge funds, proprietary traders).

TYPES OF INVESTORS

Strips enable investors to match their cash flows more closely with their liabilities; bullish investors can take positions in long strips, while long term savings institutions such as pension funds will be interested in the higher duration properties of strips. Traders can buy and sell strips for periods for which they have a view about interest rates; by conducting relative value trades in overseas strips markets they can take positions reflecting their view of rates in the UK versus these other markets. Such trading also serves to provide information on market expectations of the future direction of UK and overseas interest rates, as well as expectations on the shape of the respective yield curves.

While institutional investors will have a requirement for long-dated strips, shorter-dated strips are attractive to banks and building societies. Short-dated strips (up to five years or so in maturity) have been used to back retail products offering a guaranteed minimum return, such as a stock market-linked capital guaranteed savings account. Very short-dated strips have been used in the same way as money market instruments.

This section has broadly outlined the uses that market participants will have for strips. We have said that these will include investors and traders; the versatility of strips means that in theory there is a high demand for them. We can group the participants in buying and selling strips into the following categories:

- *Traders*: arbitrage activity, relative value trading (interest rate plays); for example a trader can sell one strip and purchase another maturing at a later date, which would lock in a forward interest rate. The trader may wish to carry out a similar trade the other way round in an overseas strips market, for instance if he had a view on interest rate convergence (or divergence);
- *Institutional investors*: pension funds and insurance companies matching future liabilities, annuities; these institutions are cash-rich and natural buyers of strips;

- *Banks and building societies*: short-term cash management and asset-liability management, money market liquidity, expressing market views, guaranteed return retail market products;
- *Central banks*: buying short-dated coupon strips as part of government cash management;
- *Money market funds*: these can use strips to reduce reinvestment risk, up to about three years maturity;
- *Corporate treasurers*: money management;
- *Hedge funds*: may wish to take advantage of high duration and convexity to trade at the very long end;
- *Foreign investors*: institutional investors may wish to express views on sterling interest rates;
- *Private investors*: mortgage redemption, school fees, retirement savings, etc.

MONEY MANAGEMENT

It is possible to lend and repo strips, as with conventional gilts, and therefore also short strips and cover such short positions via borrowing or reverse repo. Because of certain properties of strips, namely their longer duration making them more price volatile, certain market participants may prefer not deal in strips repo. However as the gilt repo market includes initial margin and (if required by a participant) daily variation margin, this should not make strips unattractive as repo collateral. The repo of gilt strips is carried out in exactly the same way as with conventional gilts, with the exception that there is no accrued interest to consider when calculating settlement amounts.

The BoE announced in April 1998 that henceforth strips would be eligible in *Delivery-by-Value* (DBV) collateral in its daily money market operations. Therefore strips have from that date been used in repo operations by the Bank.

Example 5.1: Example of Repo trade of a gilt strip

The coupon strip maturing on 7 December 2005 is repoed over a 30-day time period with the "seller" in this example providing margin of 2.5%.

Gilt strips trade on a yield basis which can then be converted into a price. If the UK Treasury Coupon Strip Dec 2005 is yielding 5.80% on 6 April 1998, then its price will be 64.497067. The repo is carried out in the normal way. Initial margin, if provided, may reflect the greater price volatility of strips compared with coupon bonds. There will obviously be no accrued interest on the collateral involved in the calculation.

If £10,000,000 nominal of the strip is repoed with an initial margin of 2.5% then the overall purchase price will be:

[10,000,000 x 0.64497067] / 1.025 = £6,292,396.78

The terms of the trade are:

Nominal	£10,000,000
Issue	Treasury Coupon Strip December 2005
Repo rate	7%
All-in price	62.923968
Purchase date	6 April
Repurchase date	6 May
Term	30 days
Total purchase consideration	£6,292,396.78
Repo interest	£36,202.83
Total repurchase consideration	6,328,599.61

If the strip maintained a yield of 5.80% throughout the trade then its price on 6 May would be 64.801708 and no margin would have been called.

Settlement

Strips settle in the same manner as conventional gilts, via the CREST system. Strips are transferable in multiples of one penny nominal value; again, this is the same as for conventional gilts. The international clearing systems Euroclear and Clearstream each have an account at CREST and therefore gilts can be settled via these clearing agents. This may be preferred by certain international investors in gilts.

THE CREST FACILITY

The original CGO settlement facility was first introduced in 1986, and upgraded in 1997 to allow for the introduction of new gilt products, namely gilt repo and strips. The CGO service is now part of CREST, the London equity market clearing system. The CGO service was originally established by the BoE and the London Stock Exchange to facilitate the settlement of specified securities, essentially Gilts and certain sterling bonds such as Bulldogs for which the BoE acts as registrar, and was upgraded by the BoE in 1997. In particular the service was upgraded to enhance gilt repo trading activity, which commenced in January 1996, and to cater for the introduction of the gilt Strips facility in December 1997. It also provides a vehicle for the development of real-time *Delivery versus Payment* (DVP) through links to the *Real Time Gross Settlement System* (RTGS) for wholesale payments, which was introduced in mid-1996.

The basic concept of CREST remains the same as that of the original CGO facility, which is the provision of secure settlement for gilt-edged securities through an efficient and reliable system of electronic book entry transfers in real time against an assured payment. CREST is a real-time, communication-based system. Settlement on the specified business day (T+1 for normal gilt trades) is dependent on the matching by CREST of correctly input and authenticated instructions by both of the parties and the successful completion of pre-settlement checks on the parties' stock account balances and credit headroom.

In 1997 the upgraded CGO provided additional features including:

- forward-dated input, useful for the input of gilt repo;
- specific capability to handle stock loans;
- greater control by settlement banks over the credit risks run on their customers (by means of a debit-capped payment mechanism);
- the movement of stock free of payment;
- transaction reporting to regulatory authorities;
- matching of instructions between counterparties;
- a flexible membership structure (allowing the names of "sponsored" as well as "direct" members to appear on the register;
- multiple account designations.

Note that firms must have an account at CREST in order to settle via the system; due to the charges involved many banks opt for an agent settlement bank to handle their transactions. It is now possible to settle gilts through Euroclear and Clearstream, both of which have accounts at CREST.

DELIVERY BY VALUE

Delivery by Value (DBV) is a mechanism whereby a CREST member may borrow money from or lend money to another CREST member against overnight gilt collateral. The CREST system automatically selects and delivers securities to a specified aggregate value on the basis of the previous night's GEMM Reference Prices; equivalent securities are returned the following business day. The DBV functionality allows the giver and taker of collateral to specify the classes of security to be included within the DBV.

DBV repo is a repo transaction in which the delivery of the securities is by the DBV mechanism in CREST; a series of DBV repos may be constructed to form an "open" or "term" DBV repo. The DBV functionality allows repo interest to be automatically calculated and paid.

STRIPS AND CREST

We have noted that strips are transferable within CREST in multiples of one penny nominal value, which is exactly the same as for conventional gilts. Strips are eligible as collateral as part of CREST'S DBV utility. As strips are in many circumstances more price volatile than coupon gilts of the same maturity, the DBV function allows both giver and taker of collateral the option of specifying the class of security that is preferred for inclusion within a DBV. Both parties must specify the same class for the delivery to settle within the system. The DBV options are:

- all classes of security held in CREST, including strips and Bulldogs;
- coupon-bearing gilts and Bulldogs;
- coupon gilts and strips;
- coupon gilts only.

Where parties have not specified an option the system will default to the first option, which will allow any type of security within

CREST to be delivered. Strips are also eligible as collateral in the BoE's daily money market operations.

Legal and Regulatory Issues

The strips market operates under the legal and regulatory framework that is described in the BoE publication "*The Official Gilt Strips Facility*" (1997). The arrangements under which gilts are stripped and reconstituted are laid out in Appendix 4 of that document. The necessary legislation enabling strips trading to begin was contained in the Finance Act 1996. Appendix 4 is known as "*The Strips Memorandum*". This confirms that strips are securities "issued" by HM Treasury under the National Loans Act (1968); holders of strips have the right, in the same way as holders of conventional gilts, to payment equal to the nominal value of the strip on the redemption date. As registered securities, coupon strips that are held to maturity are repaid under the procedures for redemption, as opposed to being handled as dividend payments. Coupon strips are therefore repaid by means of a direct payment to a CGO member's settlement bank account rather than according to any dividend payment instructions, which is the procedure that takes place with ordinary gilt coupon payments.

The rules of the London Stock Exchange were amended prior to the introduction of strips trading to recognise strips as gilt-edged securities. The rules also reflect the fact that strips are traded in the same manner as conventional gilts via the Inter-Dealer Broker service, with the proviso that the minimum size that can be posted on an IDB screen is £1 million nominal.

SUPERVISION

Firms dealing in strips are now regulated by the *Financial Services Authority* (FSA) which has taken over the regulatory and supervision duties of the *Securities and Futures Authority* (SFA), the *Investment Management Regulatory Organisation* (IMRO) and other "self-regulatory" bodies. As part of the FSA's supervision responsibility, it ensures through compliance monitoring that firms engaged in dealing have satisfactory capital adequacy requirements in place, and that these requirements cover the risks involved in trading and holding zero-coupon bonds. The FSA will also monitor that firms have sufficient risk management procedures and controls in place.

The European Union's *Capital Adequacy Directive* (CAD) introduced minimum capital requirements for those firms involved in securities business, to cover market risk and credit risk exposures. The CAD allows firms the option of selecting capital requirements calculations based on the duration of their trading book positions, or on the average maturity of their portfolio. CAD II is the later directive that allows firms to use their own trading and value-at-risk models when calculating risk capital requirements; where this option is selected the firm must apply for "model recognition" by the relevant regulatory body. In the UK this would be the BoE. Where a bank's internal model is approved for the purpose of capital calculation, the requirements are less stringent.

As they are considered for legal and supervisory purposes as identical to gilts, strips are allowable for inclusion in the liquidity requirements for banks, as stipulated by the BoE's supervision department.

THE ROLE OF THE DMO IN THE GILT MARKET

From April 1998 the responsibility for gilt issuance was taken over by the Debt Management Office (DMO). The role of the DMO covers all official operational decision-making in the gilt market. From the last quarter of 1999 the DMO will also take over the cash management for HM Government.

The DMO is an executive agency of HM Treasury. Its main objectives are to meet the annual remit for the sale of gilts, with an emphasis on minimising the cost to HM Treasury; and to promote a liquid market for gilts and gilt trading. To facilitate this the DMO attempts to conduct its operations in as transparent a way as possible, again with a view to keeping costs to the Treasury as low as possible. The DMO has also set itself further objectives that include responding to the demand for new products and providing quality customer service. As part of its remit for 1998/99 the DMO published an auction calendar, and increased the proportion of index-linked gilts that are issued as part of the total funding requirement.

In December 1998 the DMO published its framework for the future of UK government cash management, for which it assumed responsibility in 1999. The main objective for the DMO is to cover Exchequer cash flows that are anticipated from its forecasts; this will be accomplished through a structured Treasury Bill programme and also through daily money market operations. The BoE will conduct its daily money market operations in the normal manner, which involves bill and repo tenders at 09.45 and 14.30 each day. The DMO has stated that it will work to avoid clashes with the Bank's operations. The DMO's framework paper for cash management can be obtained direct, free of charge.

THE ROLE OF THE BOE IN THE GILT MARKET

Although the responsibility for UK government debt management has been transferred to the DMO, the BoE continues to maintain a link with the gilt market. The Bank is also involved in monitoring other sterling markets such as gilt futures and options, swaps, strips, gilt repo and domestic bonds. The Bank's *Quarterly Bulletin* for February 1999 listed its operational role in the gilt market as:

- calculating and publishing the coupons for index-linked gilts, after the publication of each month's inflation data and inflation index;
- setting and announcing the dividend for floating-rate gilts, which is calculated as a spread under three-month Libid each quarter.

This is in addition to the normal daily money market operations, which keeps the Bank closely connected to the gilt repo market. The BoE's dealers also carry out orders on behalf of its customers, primarily other central banks; this, connected with the above activities helps the Bank maintain a relationship with the gilt market.

Taxation

Tax reforms that would help to facilitate trading in strips were introduced prior to the introduction of both gilt repo and strips. From June 1997 the coupons on *strippable* gilts have not been subject to quarterly accounting arrangements. This served to make strips attractive investments for UK-domiciled companies. Strippable gilts pay gross coupons to all holders, which brings them into line with many overseas government bonds that also do not have a withholding tax. Those who wish to receive net coupons may request this in writing to the BoE's Registrar Department. This may be a more convenient arrangement for say, private investors who are basic rate taxpayers. By definition there is no withholding tax on strips.

GROSS COUPON PAYMENT

Companies liable to UK tax who are holders of non-strippable gilts are required to account for tax on a quarterly basis on gross gilt interest received; this usually ties in with the quarterly periods used by these companies for other purposes. Quarterly accounting does not of course apply to overseas companies or to domestic exempt companies such as pension funds. Coupons from strippable stock are not subject to the normal quarterly accounting arrangements. The legislation that is currently in place requires that tax on strippable gilts and strips is accounted for on an annual basis for those subject to UK tax. The move away from quarterly accounting for UK corporates is advantageous because of the improved cash flows that result. For example if a company has a December financial year-end, tax on a coupon payable in June 1998 would not be due until September 1999. Under the previous rules it would have been due by 15 July 1998. Holding a strippable gilt therefore grants a cash flow advantage to the corporate because of the longer period before the tax due becomes payable. Such a delay allows the company to earn interest on the tax that would have been paid under quarterly accounting.

The tax value to a company of a strippable gilt is therefore the present value of the interest earned on the tax due (but not yet payable) on each of the gilt's coupons. This serves to make strippable gilts, usually already the "benchmark" gilt for their respective maturity band (which usually results in greater liquidity compared to other gilts, which lowers yields compared to non-benchmarks), even more attractive to gilt investors compared to non-strippable gilts.

TAX IMPLICATIONS OF STRIPPING

As part of the Finance Act (1996) companies may determine their tax liability by valuing bond positions by either "marking-to-market" (valuing each position at the current market price at the close of business, with long positions marked at the bid price and short positions marked at the offer price) or on an accruals basis. Where companies use the mark-to-market method, stripping (or reconstituting) a gilt is regarded as a disposal (or purchase) of the unstripped gilt and as a purchase (disposal) of the corresponding series of strips. If a company employs the accruals basis, the stripped gilt is deemed to be disposed of at market value and the acquired strips deemed to be of total value equal to the coupon gilt. This aggregate value is allocated among the strips in proportion to the market value of the individual strips at the point of stripping. The same treatment is employed when a company reconstitutes a gilt.

The tax regime just described does not apply to non-corporates. Therefore a gilt held by an individual or a trust that is stripped is treated as being transferred with accrued interest; a gilt being reconstituted is regarded as having been acquired with interest accrued. By applying this treatment the authorities ensure that stripping and reconstituting gilts does not produce different tax liability results compared to those for holders of conventional gilts.

TAX TREATMENT OF RETURNS FROM STRIPS

There is no difference in the treatment of returns from strips compared to that of the return from conventional bonds held by corporates; the treatment of returns is identical. The total return is taxed as *income* in a company's annual tax assessment. Were the authorities to introduce stripping for index-linked gilts, the taxable return on such strips would be adjusted by an amount to account for the change in the retail price index for the year. This currently occurs with index-linked gilts.

Strips held by non-corporates are considered to be "relevant discounted securities". This means that the difference between the purchase and sale prices for the securities is subject to tax each year. The tax authority will treat holdings as if there had been a disposal and acquisition at the end of each tax year. Where individual bondholders benefit from profits made in the tax year, this is assessed as income and not capital gains, and therefore chargeable to income tax. Any losses suffered from holdings can be relieved against income earned in the same tax year. In this way the differences between the tax treatment of strips and unstripped gilts held by non-corporates is eliminated. There is also a much lower risk of any distortions occurring in the pricing of a bundle of strips compared to the price of the original strippable bond, and any resulting tax distortions are minimised.

The tax authorities are able to introduce extra rules to cover treatment of any new products introduced, such as index-linked strips, without the need to resort to new legislation.

Analysis of trading patterns

INFORMATION CONTENT OF STRIPS

The start of trading in strips has been of great interest not just to investors and traders, who are attracted by the many beneficial properties of strips, but also to market analysts and academics who can glean much new market information from the behaviour of strips in the market. For example the existence of a strips market means that we now have direct observations of zero-coupon bond yields in the gilt market. As coupon strips mature every June and December there is a wide range of observations across the yield curve. The information content of zero-coupon yield curves is used by economists, analysts and planners in corporate finance and central government and by traders in securities houses. Zero-coupon curves are often used to provide indication of market expectations of future interest rates; prior to the start of strips trading in December 1997 it was only possible to construct a theoretical zero-coupon curve for the gilt market, by deriving it from a conventional gilt yield curve.

OBSERVATIONS ON THE START OF STRIPS TRADING

At the start of trading in strips, volumes were relatively low. The market developed liquidity in a gradual manner. In the first month of trading, market turnover was approximately 2.3% of the average turnover in conventional gilts. (BoE, *QB* 2/98). At this early stage of the market, the BoE made the following observations:

- GEMMs were taking positions essentially in principal strips, generally at the medium- and long-dated ends of the curve;

- client demand had been seen in both principal and coupon strips, across the curve but mainly at the shorter and medium maturity range. The BoE suggested that this was perhaps due to the larger number and nominal value of strips at the shorter end. *(ibid)*

The BoE analysis also looked at stripping facilities in certain overseas markets. Zero-coupon bonds have existed in the United States, Canada and France for some time; they were recently introduced in Germany and are to be available shortly in Spain. Table 5.2 shows volumes outstanding in three of these countries. The data would appear to indicate that the most active strips markets are (i) relatively mature and (ii) provide large nominal outstanding values of strippable stock - as occurs in the US and France.

US, German, French and UK Strips [(a)]

	Date of start	Number of strippable stocks	Total strippable stock outstanding (billions)	Percentage stripped (by nominal value)
United States	February 1985	58	\$1,150 (£701) [(b)]	20.2%
Germany	July 1997	4	DM 102 (£34)	7.6%
France	May 1991	22	FFr 1,299 (£124)	15.3%
United Kingdom	December 1997	8	£82	1.1%

(a) Federal government stocks only. Data are as at March 1998
(b) Exchange rates as at 2 March 1998

Table 5.2 Overseas Strips Markets (Source: BoE, 1998)

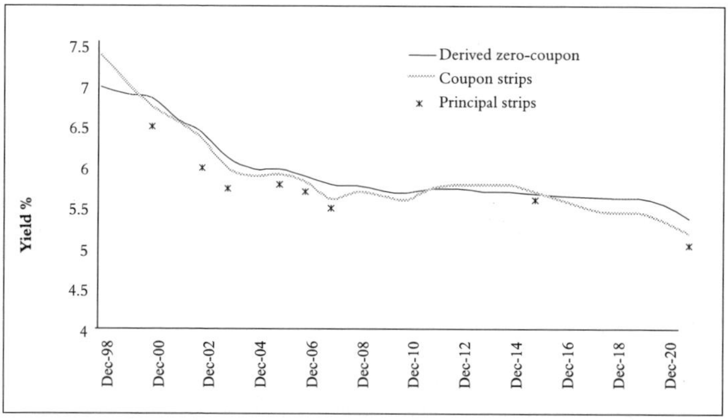

Fig 5.1 Strip Yield Curves January 1998 (Source: DMO)

It is common in strips markets for the yield curve constructed from strip price observations in the market to differ from that constructed from the conventional yield curve. Figure 5.1 shows the principal and coupon strip yield curves that existed at the start of trading in the market, as well as the theoretical zero-coupon yield curve that was derived from the benchmark yield curve. There are several reasons why spot yields quoted on strips may differ from zero-coupon yields derived from conventional gilts. A BoE analysis (*ibid*) has suggested the following such reasons:

- strip yields, like those of coupon gilts, reflect liquidity considerations. All else being equal, short coupon strips may be more liquid than longer-dated coupon strips, because of the larger volume of short-dated strips available (this is due to the accumulation of shorter-dated coupon strips from each of the individual strippable gilts, a greater potential amount than longer-dated coupon strips). For similar reasons individual strips are likely to be less liquid than benchmark conventional gilts of the same maturity;

- "segmentation effects" in the term structure of actual zero-coupon rates sometimes occurs, because demand is concentrated at particular points on the yield curve (see Chapter 3 on yield curves). For example there will be demand for short strips by market participants such as banks looking for liquidity and high credit-quality instruments, as well as demand for long-dated strips from investors such as pension funds who seek to match their long-dated liabilities. In fact these segmentation effects may have a greater impact on the strip yield curve than the conventional coupon gilt yield curve; due to the higher duration properties of strips, investors engaging in duration-matching strategies and buying long-dated strips will cause the market yield on these bonds to be lower than the yield derived from coupon gilts;
- principal strips exist in much higher nominal volumes than coupon strips of the same maturity; for this reason they are therefore more liquid and will trade at a lower yield. The BoE has suggested that the price premium for holding principal strips was around 0.5 – 3.0 basis points in yield at the start of the market. The principal strip needed to reconstitute a gilt is not fungible with any other strip, hence supply and demand influences on the *underlying* gilt will also affect the yield on the principal strip.

These are among the reasons why the observed yield curves will differ from the theoretical yield curve, and why the coupon strip curve will differ from the principal strip curve, as illustrated in Figure 5.1. Note also that the large gaps in maturity between principal strips also renders yield curve construction slightly problematic; it is not possible to observe results for a complete curve. As the number of strippable gilts increases gradually so that principal strips can exist at more points along the term structure, the accuracy and completeness of the observed yield curve will improve.

SUBSEQUENT DEVELOPMENTS AND ANALYSIS OF MARKET VOLUMES

Since the start of trading in gilt strips, activity has been low and has built up only gradually. The introduction of the new 30-year benchmark gilt, the 6% Treasury 2028 added a new potentially attractive investment instrument to the market. Although this stock was first auctioned in January 1998 it was not made strippable until May that year, when the total volume outstanding was raised to £5 billion; the BoE felt that the initial amount of £2 billion was not large enough to provide sufficient liquidity. At April 1998 the percentage of strippable stock held in stripped form stood at 2.2% (BoE, *QB*, May 1998). Turnover remained low in the first four months of trading, at an average of £135 million per week. At the time this figure represented ½% of turnover in the conventional gilt market (*ibid*). The BoE observed that a large proportion of activity involved overseas investors taking a view on sterling and exploiting arbitrage opportunities that existed between the gilt strips market and strips markets in Germany and France. The main customer interest in the early months of trading appeared to be in principal strips at the longer end of the curve, while GEMM activity would appear to be concentrated on trading principal strips against the underlying coupon gilt. This last activity is to be expected, and is the main reason that strips trading originally began in the US market. The profit potential for a government bond market maker who strips a coupon bond is mainly found in any arbitrage opportunity that results from mispricing of the underlying bond or strip. We will examine this in a later section.

There are several reasons behind the slow build-up to trading to trading in strips. A BoE analysis has suggested that these reasons include the following:

- because strips are not yet included in any industry benchmarks, there is no particular incentive for fund managers to buy and hold them (and no pressure from actuaries). An "index tracker" bond fund is more likely to buy the conventional long-dated bond;
- as we demonstrated in the section on forward rates, when the benchmark yield curve is negatively sloping, strip yields will lie below coupon bond yields, making strips look expensive relative to coupon bonds. As strips are zero-coupon instruments their duration will be longer than those of coupon gilts of the same maturity. In this environment therefore, strip yields will be closer to yields of longer-dated coupon gilts, compared to the yield on similar maturity gilts. The shape of the strips yield curve will deter some investors from holding strips because they would view them as dear to the coupon bond curve;
- as client interest in strips has remained low, activity in the professional market (between GEMMs) has also been low; lower liquidity has resulted in less competitive price quotes from GEMMs, which has increased further the cost of buying strips;
- to date the repo market in strips has been limited, which would make the financing of strips positions comparatively more costly. This may turn into something

of a vicious circle, as low liquidity in strips will lead to low volumes in strips repo, which will further make the running of strips portfolios less economically attractive. Strips market repo activity will be helped through the BoE's incorporation of strips in its daily money market operation, which made strips eligible for use as collateral via DBV. Strips have been so eligible since April 1998.

Bond markets suffered from considerable volatility and yield increases in the second half of 1998; among the factors that contributed to this was the Russian debt market collapse and financial turmoil in Brazil and east Asian emerging market economies. As is common in such circumstances, investors engaged in a "flight to quality" that traditionally shuns all but the most liquid and credit-worthy instruments. In these market conditions conventional coupon gilts were held in preference to strips, due to their greater liquidity and lower price volatility.

MARKET UPDATE

The total nominal amount of potentially strippable stock rose from £95 billion as at September 1998 to £98.5 billion at end-December 1998 (*Source: BoE*). The volume was increased after conversion in November 1998 of the (non-strippable) 8% Treasury 2009 gilt into the new 10-year strippable benchmark, the 5¾% 2009. The percentage of stock held in stripped form held at around 2½% of outstanding strippable gilts; average weekly turnover however, fell in the last quarter of 1998 from £150 million to £77 million. Strips turnover in 1998 remained steady at an average of less than ½% of turnover by value of the conventional gilts market, at around £40 million daily.

As with trading in the coupon gilt market, certain strippable gilts have been more actively stripped than others. Figure 5.2 shows stripping activity for three selected gilts.

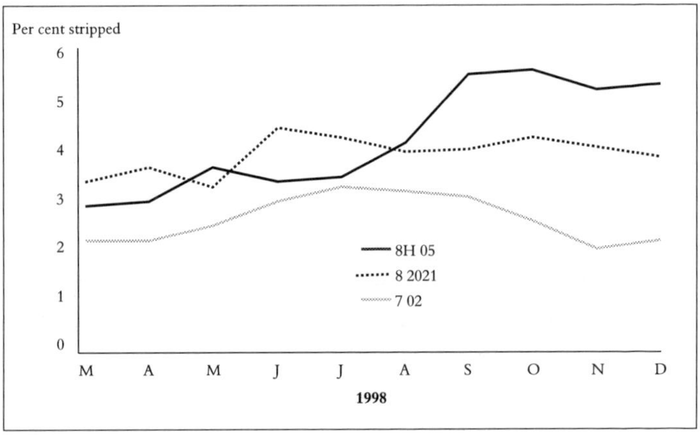

Fig 5.2 Stripping activity for three gilts (Source: BoE, 1999)

Those institutional investors buying and holding strips tend to be fund managers with an interest at the longer end of the yield curve, such as pension funds. Due to such investor demand, longer-dated gilts tend to be stripped more than short gilts. However the 8½% 2005 was also popular, with over 5% held in stripped form at December 1998 (*Source: BoE*). The principal strip from this gilt has been the highest-yielding strip beyond a maturity of five years, with a similar duration to the 7¼% 2007, which is not strippable. By holding such a strip fund managers can put on positions reflecting their view on the shape of the medium-dated part of the yield curve without affecting the duration of their portfolio.

As we noted at the start of this chapter, strips provide a direct observation of the term structure of zero-coupon interest rates. For gilts the curve constructed from strip yields is not quite a full picture, because the yields fall at only two points, and these are the same points each year. However a yield curve constructed from coupon strips is still a fairly accurate spot rate yield curve. The shape of the benchmark and strips yield curve at February 1999 is shown as Figure 5.3; for comparison the sterling swaps yield curve is also shown. We also show at Figure 5.4 the yield curves for February 1999 and August 1998; it is interesting to note that by the later date, the strips curve was trading more or less at the same level as the coupon curve. This reflected how the downturn in credit markets in the intervening period had depressed trading volumes in strips, and raised their yields accordingly. This is worth noting as the theoretical strips price given by the shape of the coupon curve had been affected by market conditions.

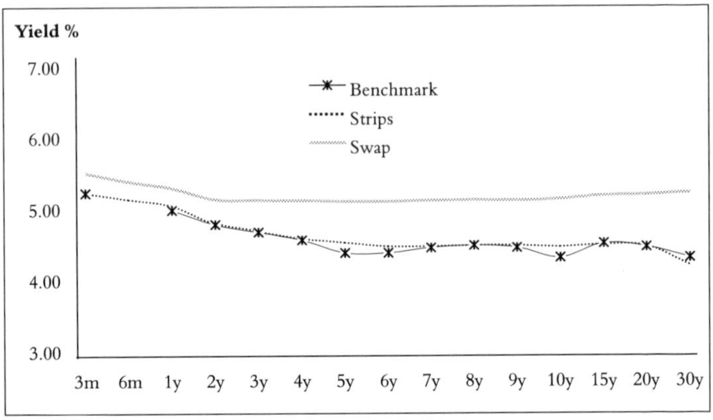

Fig 5.3 Sterling Yield Curves February 1999 (Source: Bloomberg)

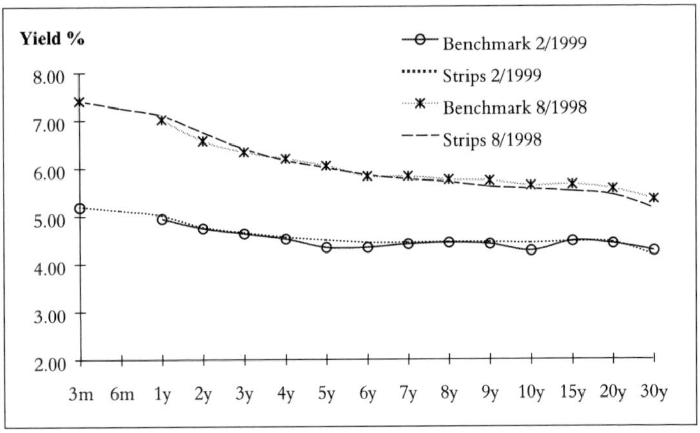

Fig 5.4 Gilt Yield Curves, August 1998 and February 1999 (Source: Bloomberg)

PRACTICAL ASPECTS

Settlement for strips essentially follows the process for cash gilts in CGO. In terms of market quotation, strips are generally quoted in yield terms in steps of 0.01%, that is 1 basis point. Under normal market conditions they trade at a bid-offer spread of around 2 basis points, but GEMMs often reserve two-way prices for selected customers only. In any case professional investors will usually ask the price only for the way they wish to trade. Illiquid strips will trade at a wider spread.

Chapter 6

ZERO-COUPON BOND TRADING STRATEGY

As we have noted elsewhere trading in strips began only gradually, and volume and liquidity levels will certainly increase as the market becomes more mature. At the start of trading transparency in the market was not as high as that in the coupon gilt market, a factor that some GEMMs were able to exploit to their advantage.

That said, strips are familiar to participants in other markets such as the USA and France, and the principles of strips trading are the same everywhere. We present here some basic concepts and strategies that are common in strips markets, and which we can expect to become the norm with gilt strips.

Strips versus coupon bonds

Before looking at trading strategies let us reiterate what was said earlier on the properties of strips. The main characteristics of strips are:

- they have a Macaulay duration equal to their maturity;
- they have no reinvestment risk because there are no intermediate cash flows;
- their prices and yields are relatively easy to calculate and require no iteration.

In theory, stripping and reconstituting a bond would be attractive if the sum value of each of the components (coupon and principal strips) is greater or less than the value of the underlying bond. Where this occurs, arbitrage profits are possible. However the market mechanism will ensure that this (almost) never happens, hence strips market participants in the UK are able to deal in an efficient and fairly priced environment.

The higher duration of strips gives them greater leverage. A smaller cash investment is required to buy a certain nominal amount compared to bonds. As strips have a much higher duration for the same calendar maturity they offer greater flexibility in matching specific cash flows. The higher convexity of strips is also an attractive feature, as convexity in a bond is a desired property. It means that the bond will appreciate more in price for a given decline in yield, than it will depreciate for the same back–up in yield. Table 6.1 is a convexity example from the German bund strips market.

Yield = 5.47%	Modified Duration	Convexity	% price change - 100bp yield	% price change +100bp yield
Bund 6.25% 2024	11.2	2.4	13.9	-11.5
Principal Strip 2024	24.9	6.4	28.4	-22.0
Coupon Strip 2010	11.2	1.6	13.1	-11.5

Table 6.1 (Arithmetic data source: Bloomberg)

Strips offer the opportunity to create strategies for a given duration with higher convexity than the equivalent coupon bond, which means strips can benefit from market volatility. This is shown in Table 6.1.

There is one further potential attraction and that is that strips can reduce currency exposure for non–sterling based investors. The increase in duration and lower price (in a positive sloping yield curve environment) of a strip relative to a similar maturity coupon gilt means that an investor can buy a smaller nominal amount of zero–coupon bonds and still maintain their desired interest rate exposure.

Determining the value of strips

It is always important to understand how strips behave under different yield curve conditions and over time; this will help the investor to identify relative value. We have already shown that the yield on a strip is predominantly a function of the shape of the yield curve, as well as related factors such as supply and demand, liquidity, market sentiment, future interest rate expectations and tax issues.

The three most common ways to calculate the value of a strip are

- valuation using the bond curve;
- equivalent duration method;
- theoretical zero–coupon curve construction, also known as *bootstrapping;*

VALUATION USING THE BOND CURVE

The spread between a strip and a bond with the same maturity is often used as an indicator of strip value. It is essentially a rough–and–ready approach; its main drawback is that two instruments with different risk profiles are being compared against each other. This is particularly true for longer maturities.

EQUIVALENT DURATION METHOD

When measuring relative value, aligning the strip and coupon bond yields on the basis of modified duration will allow for a better comparison. From Figure 5.3 it would appear that at this time strips are cheap at the short end and particularly expensive at the longer end. A proper analysis will require us to construct a curve of yields against modified duration, and check for value on such a curve. However we would have no indication as to how strip values will change for various yield curve moves.

THEORETICAL ZERO–COUPON CURVE (BOOTSTRAPPING)

This is the most common way of determining the value of a strip, via the derivation of a theoretical zero–coupon curve. We saw in

Chapter 5 how the actual strip yield curve can differ from a spot curve derived from the benchmark yield curve. When such anomalies occur there may be opportunity for profitable relative value trading. For example, a trader may wish to examine the shapes of the theoretical and actual zero–coupon curves and where they have differed from each other over time. A spread trade can be put on where an anomaly is detected, for instance where there is a greater than usual divergence of an actual yield from a theoretical yield. When the curves converge again the spread is unwound and the trader takes her profit.

A theoretical spot curve is usually calculated from a theoretical bond par yield curve (the par curve is often constructed by plotting the existing bond yields against their respective maturities, and then fitting a curve through these points using predetermined criteria). We examined in the forward rates case study how the zero–coupon or spot yield curve is then derived from a coupon curve. Strips will often trade at a spread to the theoretical zero–coupon bond value; this indicates which maturities are cheap and which expensive. And as we noted just now, in this way anomalies can be identified. In the gilt strips market, the zero–coupon curve tends to be well arbitraged on forward rates. This means that while there may well appear to be arbitrage opportunities available when analysing the spot yield curve, special repo conditions will make actual arbitrage almost impossible. This is usually taken into account in the shape of the forward curve.

SLOPE OF THE YIELD CURVE

We illustrated the relationship between coupon and zero–coupon yield curves in the case study on forward rates. When the curve is flat, the spot curve will also be flat. When the yield curve is negative, the theoretical zero–coupon curve must lie below the coupon yield curve. This is because the yield on coupon–bearing bonds is affected by the fact that the investor receives part of the cash flow before the maturity of the bond; the discount rates corresponding to these earlier payment dates are higher than the discount rate corresponding to the final payment date on redemption. In addition the spread between zero–coupon yields and bond yields should increase negatively with maturity, so that zero–coupon bonds always yield less than coupon bonds.

In a positively shaped yield curve environment the opposite is true. The theoretical zero–coupon curve will lie above the coupon curve. It is interesting however to observe the overall steepness of the curves. In general the steeper the coupon curve is, the steeper the zero–coupon curve will be. It should be remembered that each yearly value of the coupon curve is considered in the derivation of the zero–coupon curve. Hence a yield curve could for example, have only one–year, 10–year and 30–year yields, while the theoretical zero–coupon 30–year yield could be substantially higher or lower. The derived yield level would depend on whether the points on the term structure in between these maturity bands were connected by a smooth curve or straight line.

This argument is sometimes cited as a reason for not using the bootstrapping method, in that the theoretical zero–coupon yields that are obtained are too sensitive for real–world trading. Bond analysts often use sophisticated curve smoothing techniques to get around this problem, and produce theoretical values that are more realistic. This issue becomes more important when there are few bonds between distant points on the term structure, such that linear interpolation between them produces more inaccurate results.

For example between the ten–year and thirty–year maturities there are eight liquid gilts; between twenty and thirty years there are only two gilts.

Strips Market Anomalies

From the start of gilt strips trading the market has observed some long–standing anomalies that mirror observations from other strips markets, such as those in the USA and France. These include the following:

FINAL PRINCIPAL TRADES EXPENSIVE

It might be expected that the strip yield curve would behave in a similar fashion to the coupon curve. However due to supply and demand considerations more weight is always given to the final principal strip, and this is indeed so in the gilt strips market.

LONGEST MATURITY IS THE MOST EXPENSIVE

A characteristic seen in all well–developed strip markets is that maturities with the longest duration and the greatest convexity trade expensive relative to theoretical values. Conversely, intermediate maturities tend to trade cheap to the curve. This can be observed when looking at the gilt strips and coupon curves.

PRINCIPAL STRIPS TRADE AT A PREMIUM OVER COUPON STRIPS

Principal strips reflect the premium investors are prepared to pay for greater liquidity and, in some markets, for regulatory and tax reasons. This rule is so well established that principal strips will sometimes trade more expensive relative to coupon strips even when their outstanding nominal amount is lower than that of coupon strips.

INTERMEDIATE MATURITY COUPONS ARE OFTEN RELATIVELY CHEAP

Market makers in the past have often found themselves with large quantities of intermediate maturity coupon strips, the residue of client demand for longer maturities. This has occurred with gilt strips where at certain times coupon strips of 3–8 years maturity have traded cheap to the curve.

VERY SHORT COUPON STRIPS TRADE EXPENSIVE

In a positively sloped yield curve environment short strips are often in demand because they provide an attractive opportunity to match liabilities without reinvestment risk at a higher yield than coupon bonds of the same maturity. We have not observed this in the gilt strips market to date, as the yield curve has been inverted from before the start of trading. However in France for example the short end up to three years is often well bid.

Trading Strategy

BOND REPLICATION THROUGH STRIPS

This is the theoretical strategy and the one that first presents itself. The profit potential for a GEMM who strips a gilt lies in arbitrage resulting from a mispricing of the coupon bond. Due to the market mechanism requiring that there be no arbitrage opportunity, the bid price of a gilt must be lower than the offer price of a synthetic gilt (a gilt reconstituted from a bundle of coupon and principal strips); equally the offer price of the gilt must be higher than the bid price of a synthetic gilt. Of course if the above conditions are not satisfied, a risk–free profit can be obtained by trading the opposite way in both instruments simultaneously and simply taking the difference.

The potential profit in stripping a gilt will depend on actual gilt yields prevailing in the market and the theoretical spot rate yield curve. To illustrate how a GEMM might realise a profit from a coupon stripping exercise, consider a hypothetical five–year, 8 per cent gilt selling at par (and therefore offering a yield to maturity of 8%). Let us imagine that the GEMM buys the gilt at par and strips it, with the intention of selling the resulting zero–coupon bonds at the yields indicated for the corresponding maturity shown in Table 6.2. The table shows prices and yields for a group of hypothetical gilts, and assumes a settlement date of 1 March 1999, which is a coupon date, so that each of the bonds has precisely 0.5, 1, 1.5 and so on years to maturity. The theoretical spot rates shown have been calculated using the coupon yields and the *bootstrapping* method.

Maturity Date	Years to maturity	Yield to Maturity (%)	Theoretical Spot Rate (%)
1-Sep-99	0.5	6.00	6.000
1-Mar-00	1.0	6.30	6.308
1-Sep-00	1.5	6.40	6.407
1-Mar-01	2.0	6.70	6.720
1-Sep-01	2.5	6.90	6.936
1-Mar-02	3.0	7.30	7.394
1-Sep-02	3.5	7.60	7.712
1-Mar-03	4.0	7.80	7.908
1-Sep-03	4.5	7.95	8.069
1-Mar-04	5.0	8.00	8.147

Table 6.2

The yield curves for these rates are shown as Figure 6.1.

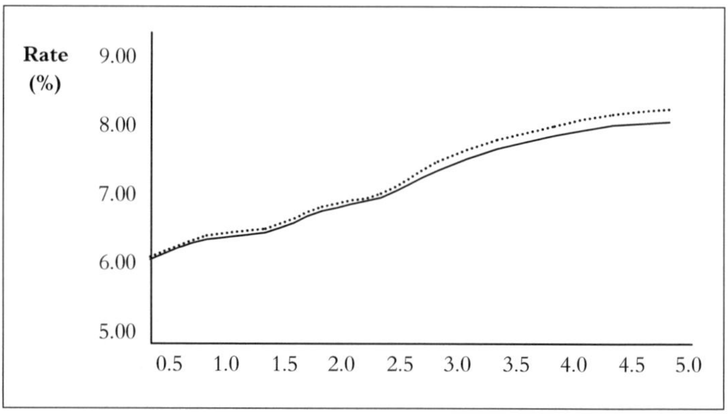

Fig 6.1

Table 6.3 shows the price that the GEMM would receive for each strip that was created. As we saw in Chapter 1 the price of the coupon gilt is the discounted total present value of all its cash flows using the required market interest rate. Here we can equate it to the total present value of all the cash flows from the strips, each discounted at the yield corresponding to its maturity (from Table 6.2). The proceeds received from selling the strips come to a total of £100.4913 per £100 of par value of the gilt originally bought by the GEMM.

Maturity Date	**Years to Maturity**	**Cash Flow**	**Present Value at 8%**	**Yield to Maturity (%)**	**Present Value at Yield to Maturity**
1-Sep-99	0.5	4	3.8462	6.00	3.8835
1-Mar-00	1.0	4	3.6982	6.30	3.7594
1-Sep-00	1.5	4	3.5560	6.40	3.6393
1-Mar-01	2.0	4	3.4192	6.70	3.5060
1-Sep-01	2.5	4	3.2877	6.90	3.3760
1-Mar-02	3.0	4	3.1613	7.30	3.2258
1-Sep-02	3.5	4	3.0397	7.60	3.0809
1-Mar-03	4.0	4	2.9228	7.80	2.9453
1-Sep-03	4.5	4	2.8103	7.95	2.8164
1-Mar-04	5.0	104	70.2587	8.00	70.2587
			100.0000		100.4913

Table 6.3

We can analyse why the GEMM has had the opportunity to realise this profit. Consider the fourth column in Table 6.3. This shows us how much the GEMM paid for each of the cash flows by buying the entire package of cash flows, that is, by buying the bond at a yield of 8%. For instance let us examine the £4 coupon payment due in three years. By buying the five–year gilt priced to yield 8%, the GEMM pays a price based on 8% (4% semi–annual) for that coupon payment, which is £3.1613. However if we accept the assumptions in this illustration, investors are willing to accept a lower yield, 7.30% (3.65% semi–annual) and purchase a strip with three years to maturity at the price marked. Note that the present value calculation uses equation 6.1 which is the standard discounted cash flow equation, adjusted for bonds paying semi–annual coupons.

$$PV = \frac{FV}{\left(1+\frac{r}{2}\right)^{nm}}$$

(6.1)

where n is the number of years in the term (years to maturity), r is the bond yield to maturity and m is the number of compounding periods per year.

Thus investors here are willing to pay £3.2258. On this one coupon payment (now of course a strip versus a coupon payment) the GEMM realises a profit equal to the difference between £3.2258 and £3.1613, or £0.0645. From all the strips the total profit is £0.4913 per £100 nominal.

Maturity Date	Years to Maturity	Cash Flow	Present Value at 8%	Theoretical Spot Rate (%)	Present Value at Spot Rate
1-Sep-99	0.5	4	3.8462	6.000	3.8835
1-Mar-00	1.0	4	3.6982	6.308	3.7591
1-Sep-00	1.5	4	3.5560	6.407	3.6390
1-Mar-01	2.0	4	3.4192	6.720	3.5047
1-Sep-01	2.5	4	3.2877	6.936	3.3731
1-Mar-02	3.0	4	3.1613	7.394	3.2171
1-Sep-02	3.5	4	3.0397	7.712	3.0693
1-Mar-03	4.0	4	2.9228	7.908	2.9331
1-Sep-03	4.5	4	2.8103	8.069	2.8020
1-Mar-04	5.0	104	70.2587	8.147	69.7641
			100.0000		~100.0000

Table 6.4

Let us now imagine that instead of the observed yield to maturity from Table 6.3, the yields required by investors are the same as the theoretical spot rates also shown. Table 6.4 shows that in this case the total proceeds from the sale of zero–coupon gilts would be approximately £100, which being no profit would render the exercise of stripping uneconomic. This shows that where strips prices deviate from theoretical prices, there may be profit opportunities. We have shown elsewhere that there are differences between observed strip yields and theoretical yields, indicating that there are (often very small) differences between derived prices and actual prices. Do these price differences give rise to arbitrage opportunities? Due to the efficiency and transparency of developed country bond markets, the answer is usually no. It is the process of coupon stripping that prevents the price of a gilt from trading at a price that is *materially* different from its theoretical price based on the derived spot yield curve. And where discrepancies arise, any arbitrage activity will cause them to disappear very quickly. As the strips market becomes more liquid, the laws of supply and demand will eliminate obvious arbitrage opportunities, as has already happened in the US Treasury market and is already the norm in the gilts market. However there will remain occasional opportunities to exploit differences between actual market prices of strips and the theoretical price given by the benchmark (coupon) gilt yield curve.

TRACKING THEORETICAL SPREADS

Anomalies can sometimes be detected by tracking the spreads of strips against the theoretical yield curve. As noted earlier, supply and demand considerations make a strip that is not in demand trade at cheaper levels. This may induce an investor to buy the strip. Conversely a strip that is in demand will become expensive and thus, might signal a selling opportunity when compared to the average levels it has traded at historically.

ROLLING DOWN THE CURVE

In a positive yield curve environment strips will give a superior return due to a greater "roll-down" effect, since the zero–coupon curve will stand higher than the par curve, especially at short maturities. On the other hand when a change in monetary policy is anticipated, switching into long duration strips will provide greater leverage and price performance.

DURATION WEIGHTED SWITCHES

It is very important to ensure that the risk profile of a portfolio or position remains the same when switching from bonds into strips (assuming that the current interest rate risk exposure is what is desired). This can be achieved by duration–weighting the new portfolio made up of the strips (and cash). Table 6.5 gives three hypothetical examples of duration weighted switches for gilts and strips with assumed prices and yield values in a positive yield curve environment.

	Nominal	**Cash**	**Deposit**	**Yield**
(1) Bond into strip: same maturity				
Sell				
Gilt 5.75% 2009	100	100	0	5.75
Buy				
Principal strip 2009	129	75	25	5.98
(2) Bond into strip: longer maturity				
Sell				
Gilt 5.75% 2009	100	100	0	5.75
Buy				
Principal strip 2021	356	59	41	7.14
(3) Bond into strip: shorter maturity				
Sell				
Gilt 5.75% 2009	100	100	0	5.75
Buy				
Coupon strip June 2002	288	262	-162 (borrow)	3.83

Table 6.5 Duration weighed switches

BARBELL STRATEGIES

A *barbell* strategy involves selling an intermediate maturity coupon bond and using the proceeds to buy a duration–weighted combination of both shorter– and longer–duration bonds. The opposite to this position is called a *butterfly*. Barbell strategies have two advantages:

- barbells increase the holding period return;
- barbells may increase the convexity of the portfolio.

To achieve a possible yield pick–up in a positive yield curve environment, an investor could sell the long gilt (2028 maturity) and buy both the five–year gilt and the long strip to pick up yield while maintaining the same exposure to the market with the help of the high duration strip. However in a negative yield curve environment, which prevailed in the gilt market at the time of writing, this strategy is not possible. We have illustrated this strategy using a set of yields that existed in the German bund and strips market in July 1998, shown in Table 6.6.

Sell 26-year bond, buy 5-year bond and 25-year strip

	Cash	**Mod Dur**	**Yield**
Sell 6.25% Jan 2024	1,000	12.2	6.47
Buy 6% Sept 2003	0.603	4.9	4.96
Buy July 2023 strip	0.397	23.4	9.27
Duration weighted yield pick-up			14bp

Table 6.6

The relative performance of the barbell is evidently subject to second–order yield curve risk. If the shape of the curve changes the performance of the position will be affected. For example if the yield curve steepens, that is the yield spread between the short–dated maturity and long–dated maturity widens, the barbell would benefit; if the curve flattens the butterfly would probably outperform.

PORTFOLIO OPTIMISATION

Strips are attractive for cash flow matching of assets with specific liabilities, or for enhancing the portfolio yield through duration matching.

CROSS–CURRENCY SPREADS

As we have already noted, the high duration characteristic of strips means that less cash is needed to invest in a market to retain the same exposure to yield moves, giving less currency exposure compared to holding coupon bonds. Table 6.7 shows an hypothetical example, in a positive yield curve environment, of a US dollar–based investor who is holding the 5¾% Treasury 2009 gilt, but wishes to reduce his currency risk. By switching out of the bonds into a duration–weighted amount of 15–year strips and cash (surplus funds are deposited in short–term cash accounts), the investor has reduced his currency risk while still being able to benefit from a fall in sterling interest rates. Part of the currency risk has been exchanged for yield curve exposure.

	Cash	Nominal	Mod Dur	Yield
5.75% 2009	100	100	7.0	5.68
$ cash (1y)	50	53	0.0	6.00
Strip 2015	50	120	14.1	6.33
weighted yield pick-up				14bp

Table 6.7 Cross–currency trade example

CURRENCY PROTECTION

During periods of high currency volatility, investors may wish to reduce their exposure to a certain currency but maintain an interest rate exposure in that currency's bond market. This can be achieved by switching from bonds into strips, and releasing the cash from this switch into assets of a currency that is perceived to be more stable. The position can be switched back when the period of currency volatility passes. The ability to take a long position in a market while limiting currency exposure will also reduce the hedging cost of the position.

Chapter 7

EXAMPLE: YIELD AND CASH FLOW ANALYSIS

The following examples illustrate the yield analysis and cash flows for the 5¾% Treasury 2009, which matures on 7 December 2009, its principal strip and a coupon strip maturing on 7 December 2009. The 5¾% 2009 is the current ten–year benchmark gilt. The market information reflects the position as at February 1999, for settlement date 11 February 1999. Interest rate and price data was obtained from Bloomberg and Reuters.

Table 7.1 below shows the cash flows paid out to a bondholder of £1 million nominal of the 5¾% 2009. On the trade date (10 February 1999, for settlement on 11 February) this bond traded at 113.15, with a corresponding yield of 4.2224%. The convexity of this bond at this time was 0.820. The relevant spot rates at each of the cashflow dates are shown alongside. A graph of the spot curve is given in Figure 7.1.

PAY DATE	CASH FLOW	SPOT	PAY DATE	CASH FLOW	SPOT
7-Jun-99	28,750.00	5.1474	7-Dec-04	28,750.00	4.2746
7-Dec-99	28,750.00	4.9577	7-Jun-05	28,750.00	4.3168
7-Jun-00	28,750.00	4.8511	7-Dec-05	28,750.00	4.3599
7-Dec-00	28,750.00	4.7376	7-Jun-06	28,750.00	4.3738
7-Jun-01	28,750.00	4.6413	7-Dec-06	28,750.00	4.3881
7-Dec-01	28,750.00	4.5481	7-Jun-07	28,750.00	4.3603
7-Jun-02	28,750.00	4.4614	7-Dec-07	28,750.00	4.3326
7-Dec-02	28,750.00	4.3962	7-Jun-08	28,750.00	4.2942
7-Jun-03	28,750.00	4.3307	7-Dec-08	28,750.00	4.2548
7-Dec-03	28,750.00	4.2654	7-Jun-09	28,750.00	4.2153
7-Jun-04	28,750.00	4.2696	7-Dec-09	28,750.00	4.1759

Nominal	1,000,000	Previous coupon date	7-Dec-98
Duration	8.33	Accrued Interest	10,425.82
Total Cashflow	1,632,500.00	Present Value	1,141,925.84

Table 7.1 Cashflow Analysis Treasury 5 ¾% 2009, yield 4.2224% February 1999 (Source: Bloomberg)

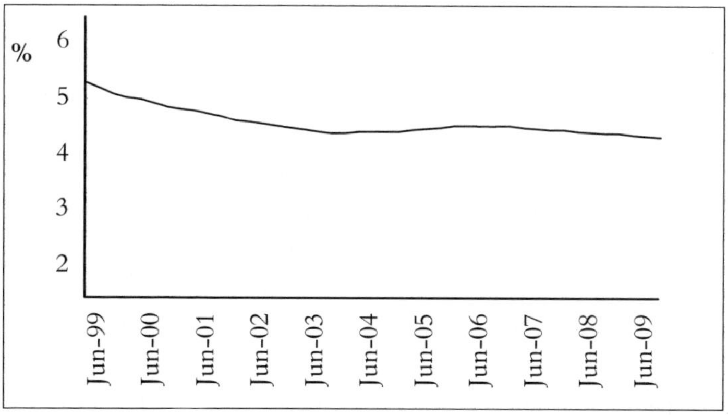

Fig 7.1

The cash flow for the December 2009 principal strip is shown as table 7.2. Note that if calling up this security on the Bloomberg system, the "ticker" is UKTR, comprising the standard UKT (from "United Kingdom Treasury") and the suffix R (from "residual", the Bloomberg term for principal strips). The Bloomberg ticker for coupon strips is UKTS.

The yield on the principal strip at this time was 4.1482%, which corresponds to a price of 64.13409 per £100 nominal. Given that the yield curve was inverted at this time, this is what is expected, a yield lower than the gross redemption yield for the coupon gilt. For a holding of £1 million nominal there is only one cash flow, the redemption payment of £1 million on the redemption date. The convexity for the principal strip was 1.175, which illustrates the higher convexity property of strips versus coupon bonds. Comparing the tables we can see also that duration for the strip is higher than that for the coupon gilt. Note the analysis for the principal strip gives us a slightly different spot curve.

PAY DATE	CASH FLOW	SPOT	PAY DATE	CASH FLOW	SPOT
7-Jun-99	0.00	5.1835	7-Dec-04	0.00	4.2683
7-Dec-99	0.00	4.9577	7-Jun-05	0.00	4.3102
7-Jun-00	0.00	4.8509	7-Dec-05	0.00	4.3529
7-Dec-00	0.00	4.7373	7-Jun-06	0.00	4.3672
7-Jun-01	0.00	4.6411	7-Dec-06	0.00	4.3821
7-Dec-01	0.00	4.5480	7-Jun-07	0.00	4.3571
7-Jun-02	0.00	4.4613	7-Dec-07	0.00	4.3322
7-Dec-02	0.00	4.3952	7-Jun-08	0.00	4.2937
7-Jun-03	0.00	4.3290	7-Dec-08	0.00	4.2543
7-Dec-03	0.00	4.2629	7-Jun-09	0.00	4.2148
7-Jun-04	0.00	4.2651	7-Dec-09	1,000,000.00	4.1753

Nominal	1,000,000	Previous coupon date	7-Dec-98
Duration	10.82	Accrued Interest	0.00
Total Cashflow	1,000,000.00	Present Value	641,340.87

Table 7.2 Cashflow Analysis Treasury 5¾% 2009 Principal Strip, yield 4.1482% February 1999 (Source: Bloomberg)

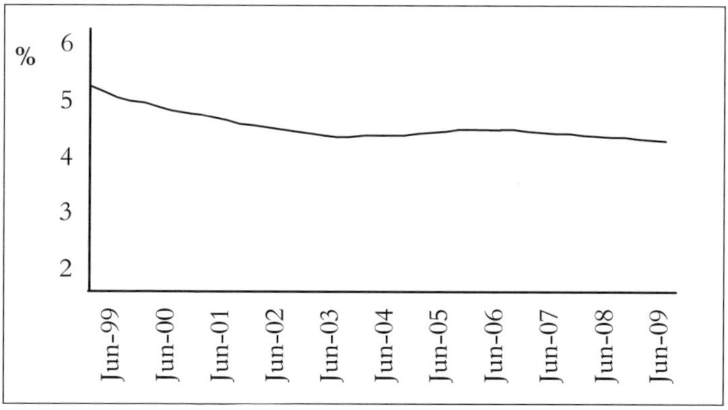

Fig 7.2

Finally we show in Table 7.3 the cashflow analysis for a coupon strip maturing on 7 December 2009. The yield quote for this coupon strip at this time was 4.4263%, corresponding to a price of 62.26518 per £100 nominal. This illustrates the point on strip prices we referred to earlier; according to a strict interpretation of the law of one price, all strips maturing on the same date should have the same price (the question being asked is, why should an investor have a different yield requirement depending on whether the £100 nominal he receives on maturity was once interest or once principal?). However as we have already stated, the liquidity differences between principal and coupon strips makes the former easier to trade and also more sought after by investors, hence the difference in yield between principal and coupon strip. The more liquid instrument trades at the lower yield.

PAY DATE	CASH FLOW	SPOT	PAY DATE	CASH FLOW	SPOT
7-Jun-99	0.00	5.2025	7-Dec-04	0.00	4.3217
7-Dec-99	0.00	5.0151	7-Jun-05	0.00	4.3672
7-Jun-00	0.00	4.8927	7-Dec-05	0.00	4.4136
7-Dec-00	0.00	4.7633	7-Jun-06	0.00	4.4353
7-Jun-01	0.00	4.6881	7-Dec-06	0.00	4.4576
7-Dec-01	0.00	4.6108	7-Jun-07	0.00	4.4299
7-Jun-02	0.00	4.5138	7-Dec-07	0.00	4.4023
7-Dec-02	0.00	4.4450	7-Jun-08	0.00	4.3608
7-Jun-03	0.00	4.3761	7-Dec-08	0.00	4.3183
7-Dec-03	0.00	4.3074	7-Jun-09	0.00	4.2758
7-Jun-04	0.00	4.3141	7-Dec-09	1,000,000.00	4.2333

Nominal	1,000,000	Previous coupon date	7-Dec-98
Duration	10.82	Accrued Interest	0.00
Total Cashflow	1,000,000.00	Present Value	622,651.18

Table 7.3 Cashflow Analysis, December 2009 Coupon Strip, yield 4.4263% February 1999, (Source: Bloomberg)

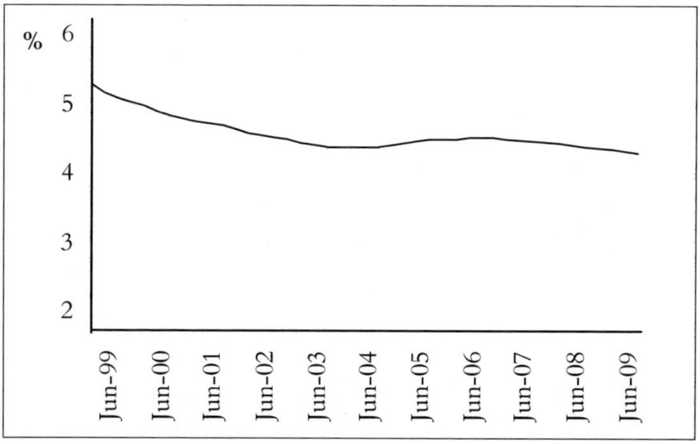
%
6
5
4
3
2
Jun-99
Jun-00
Jun-01
Jun-02
Jun-03
Jun-04
Jun-05
Jun-06
Jun-07
Jun-08
Jun-09

Fig 7.3

Chapter 8

FUTURE DEVELOPMENTS

The strips market is still a relatively new market and there remains the possibility of exciting new products being introduced at some point in the future. The BoE and DMO are in regular consultation with the market as part of their normal business activity in gilts, and should there be a large demand for new developments then we can expect to see new instruments being introduced. Products that have already been mooted include deferred payment gilts, which would not make coupon payments for a set period after issue, and annuities, which would comprise a stream of coupon payments, with no principal repayment at maturity. The BoE has stated that investors can create these instruments themselves from within the existing strips facility. For example investors could use strips to create a synthetic deferred payment gilt or annuity by acquiring strips that provide cash flows for specific points in the future. Alternatively investors could purchase the entire term of cash flows from a stripped gilt and then sell the strips that were not required. For similar reasons the BoE (and now the DMO) decided against direct issuance of strips, alongside the strips facility. At present time it is uncertain to what extent demand exists for such direct issue, and what the pattern of demand would be. In any case the current arrangements are sufficient to meet demand, rendering it unnecessary for the central authorities to analyse and identify what this demand is.

Before the start of trading, the BoE consulted with the market on the need for a second pair of coupon dates in addition to the planned and subsequently introduced pair of 7 June and 7 December. An extra set of cash flow dates would increase investor choice. However it was felt at the time that it may reduce available volume and hence liquidity, and therefore was not introduced. This issue remains under consideration, as either a possibility for only the short end of the market, or along the yield curve, and may be introduced should liquidity build up and sufficient demand be deemed to exist.

In the BoE's original consultation paper on the strips market, the possibility of issuing index–linked strips was raised. Certain investment institutions (generally long–dated bond investors such as pension funds, who currently also invest in coupon index–linked gilts) have expressed interest in such instruments. Allowing the market to strip indexed bonds would enable them to create inflation–linked products that are more tailored to clients' needs, such as indexed annuities or deferred payment indexed bonds. In overseas markets where stripping of indexed government bonds does take place, the resulting strip is an individual uplifted cash flow. An interesting development has taken place in New Zealand, where the cash flows are separated into three components: the principal, the principal inflation adjustment and the set of inflation–linked coupons (that is, an indexed annuity). In the UK however it is felt that the small issue size of index–linked gilts and their coupons would result in a strips market of very low liquidity. The authorities have stated that the case for index–linked gilts will be reviewed in the light of experience gained with conventional strips; indeed all possibilities are under constant review and may be introduced if the market develops a significant demand for these types of instruments. Hence as the gilt strips market develops we can expect to see new developments and possibly new structures being introduced. If this contributes to maintaining the attraction of gilts to domestic and overseas investors it will be to the advantage of sterling market liquidity as a whole.

GLOSSARY

Actual/365

This is a day count convention used in the bond markets as part of the accrued interest calculation for bonds paying semi–annual interest. It calculates the period since the last dividend date by dividing the actual number of days that elapsed by 182.5, that is, 365 divided by 2.

Actual/actual

This convention calculates the period since the last dividend date by dividing the actual number of days that have elapsed by the actual number of days in the dividend period.

All–in price

See "dirty price".

Annuity

A continuous yearly stream of fixed payments.

Bid

The price at which a market maker will buy stock in the market, one side of the bid–offer quote.

Bootstrapping
The term used to describe a method for deriving the spot (zero–coupon) curve from the coupon or par yield curve.

Bulldog
Sterling domestic bonds issued by non–UK domiciled borrowers. These bonds trade under a similar arrangement to Gilts and are settled via the Central Gilts Office.

Central Gilts Office (CGO)
The office of the Bank of England which runs the computer–based settlement system for gilt–edged securities and certain other securities (mostly Bulldogs) for which the Bank acts as Registrar. Merged with CREST in July 2000.

CGO reference prices
Daily prices of gilt–edged and other securities held in CGO which are used by CGO in various processes, including revaluing stock loan transactions, calculating total consideration in a repo transaction, and DBV assembly. Now known as *DMO prices* or *gilt reference prices*.

Cheap to the curve
A bond whose yield is above the point on the yield curve where, given its maturity, the yield would be expected to lie, is said to be trading "cheap to the curve".

Convexity
The rate of change of modified duration with yield/price, effectively the second derivative of the change in price of a bond with respect to yield.

Corpus
An alternative name for principal strip.

Day Count
The convention used to calculate accrued interest on bonds and interest on cash. For UK gilts the convention changed to actual/actual from actual/365 on 1 November 1998. For cash the convention in sterling markets is actual/365.

DBV (delivery by value)
A mechanism whereby a CGO member may borrow from or lend money to another CGO member against overnight gilt collateral. The CGO system automatically selects and delivers securities to a specified aggregate value on the basis of the previous night's CGO reference prices; equivalent securities are returned the following day. The DBV functionality allows the giver and taker of collateral to specify the classes of security to included within the DBV. The options are: all classes of security held within CGO, including strips and bulldogs; coupon bearing gilts and bulldogs; coupon bearing gilts and strips; only coupon bearing gilts.

Debt Management Office (DMO)
The DMO was set up to manage the government's debt issuance programme, which it took over from the BoE in April 1998. It is an executive agency of HM Treasury.

Delivery versus payment (DVP)
The simultaneous exchange of securities and cash. The assured payment mechanism of the CGO achieves the same protection.

Dirty price

The price of a bond including accrued interest. Also known as the "all–in" price.

Duration

The weighted average time to receipt of cashflows from a financial instrument. *Modified duration*, derived from the duration measure, is a measure of the sensitivity of a bond's price to a change in its yield.

Duration weighting

The process of using the modified duration value for bonds to calculate the exact nominal holdings in a spread position. This is necessary because £1 million nominal of a two–year bond is not equivalent to £1 million of say, a five–year bond. The modified duration value of the five–year bond will be higher, indicating that its "basis point value" (bpv) will be greater, and that therefore £1 million worth of this bond represents greater sensitivity to a move in interest rates (risk). As another example consider a fund manager holding £10 million of five–year bonds. The fund manager wishes to switch into a holding of two–year bonds with the same overall risk position. The basis point values of the bonds are 0.041583 and 0.022898 respectively. The ratio of the bpvs are 0.041583 / 0.022898 = 1.816. The fund manager therefore needs to switch into £10m x 1.816 = £18.160 million of the two–year bond.

Ex–dividend (*xd*) date

A bond's record date for the payment of coupons. The coupon payment will be made to the person who is the registered holder of the stock on the *xd* date. For gilts this is seven working days before the coupon date.

Fungibility

The ability to combine coupon cashflows occurring on the same date even if they have been created from different bonds. Principal cashflows (strips) from different bonds are not fungible, and nor are principal and coupon strips.

GEMM

A Gilt–Edged Market Maker; these are securities houses and investment banks registered as market makers in gilts with the Bank of England. GEMMs are required to make continuous two–way prices in all but the most illiquid gilts at all times, in return for which they are granted certain dealing privileges by the Bank.

ISIN

This is the internationally recognised securities identifier, from *International Security Identification Number*, a 12–digit number that incorporates the 7–digit SEDOL (*Stock Exchange Daily Official List*) number for UK securities, including gilts.

Libid

The London Interbank Bid Rate, the rate at which banks will pay for money amongst themselves, that is in the interbank market.

Libor

The London Interbank Offered Rate, the lending rate for all major currencies up to one–year set at 11am each day by the British Bankers Association.

LIFFE

The London International Financial Futures Exchange, based in Canon Bridge in London. A major exchange for trading in derivative contracts including the medium– and long–gilt futures contracts.

Offer
The price at which a market maker will sell stock, one side of the bid–offer quote.

Parallel shift
A parallel shift is a change in the level of the yield curve, where all points along the yield curve move by exactly the same amount. For example a 10 basis point upward parallel shift in the yield curve means that all points along the term structure (all maturity points) have moved up in yield by 10 basis point. By definition this means that the shape of the yield curve remains the same after the parallel shift has taken place.

Primary market
The market for newly issued capital market securities; bonds issue for the first time are being bought by investors in the primary market.

Principal
A zero–coupon bond created when coupons are stripped from a conventional bond; the principal is the residual redemption payment that is paid, at par, on the bond's maturity date. The zero–coupon bonds that result from the coupons are known as *coupon strips.*

Quarterly accounting
The arrangement whereby withholding tax on coupons is paid shortly after the end of the calendar quarter.

Quasi–coupon date
The date on which a coupon would be due on a bond assuming it is a conventional bond and not a strip.

Reconstitution
The process of reconstituting a bond from its component cash-flows.

Repo
A collateralised loan, the term originates from *sale and repurchase agreement*, under which a bond holder "sells" a bond with a simultaneous agreement to repurchase the bond on an agreed date. The bond serves as security for the cash that is received by the bond "seller", on returning the funds the bond holder will pay interest at the agreed repo rate.

Repo rate
The return earned on a repo transaction expressed as an interest rate on the cash side of the transaction.

Secondary market
Capital market securities including bonds, being bought and sold after their initial issue are said to be trading in the *secondary market*. The *primary market* is the market into which instruments are first sold (issued).

Spline method
The method by which a par yield curve is modelled, based on a series of polynomial equations spliced together.

Strip
A zero–coupon bond which is produced by separating a standard coupon–bearing bond into its constituent principal and interest components. Originates from the expression *Separate Trading of Registered Interest and Principal of Securities*.

Term repo
Repo trades (of a maturity over one day) with a fixed maturity date.

Vasicek method
The method by which a zero–coupon yield curve is modelled, based on statistical methodology.

Withholding tax
Income tax deducted at source from gilt coupon payments.

APPENDICES

Appendix I

Gilt Strips as at 2 March 1999 (C – coupon; P – principal)

Strip	Price	Yield	Modified Duration	Convexity
Jun-99 C	98.692	5.068	0.26	0.002
Dec-99 C	96.355	4.918	0.75	0.009
Jun-00 C	93.930	5.009	1.23	0.021
Dec-00 P	91.586	5.036	1.72	0.038
Dec-00 C	91.685	4.973	1.72	0.038
Jun-01 C	89.462	4.976	2.21	0.060
Dec-01 C	87.348	4.949	2.7	0.086
Jun-02 P	85.467	4.867	3.19	0.117
Jun-02 C	85.350	4.910	3.19	0.117
Dec-02C	83.426	4.861	3.68	0.154
Jun-03 C	81.581	4.824	4.17	0.194
Dec-03 P	80.158	4.691	4.66	0.240
Dec-03 C	79.805	4.786	4.66	0.240
Jun-04 C	77.897	4.798	5.15	0.290
Dec-04 C	76.067	4.798	5.63	0.345
Jun-05 C	74.355	4.783	6.12	0.405
Dec-05 P	72.819	4.740	6.61	0.470
Dec-05 C	72.661	4.774	6.61	0.469
Jun-06 C	70.960	4.776	7.1	0.539
Dec-06 C	69.278	4.781	7.59	0.613
Dec-06 P	69.304	4.775	7.59	0.613
Jun-07 C	67.747	4.765	8.08	0.692
Dec-07 C	66.237	4.753	8.57	0.776
Dec-07 P	66.408	4.723	8.57	0.776
Jun-08 C	64.798	4.733	9.06	0.866
Dec-08 C	63.287	4.735	9.55	0.959
Jun-09 C	61.852	4.731	10.04	1.056
Dec-09 P	61.804	4.518	10.53	1.161
Dec-09 C	60.479	4.723	10.52	1.159
Jun-10 C	59.167	4.711	11.01	1.266
Dec-10 C	57.798	4.711	11.5	1.379
Jun-11 C	56.460	4.713	11.99	1.496
Dec-11 C	55.152	4.713	12.48	1.618
Jun-12 C	53.881	4.713	12.97	1.745
Dec-12 C	52.640	4.713	13.46	1.877

(Source: Bloomberg, HSBC)

Strip	Price	Yield	Modified Duration	Convexity
Jun-13 C	51.427	4.714	13.950	2.013
Dec-13 C	50.278	4.706	14.440	2.156
Jun-14C	49.128	4.706	14.930	2.301
Dec-14 C	48.012	4.705	15.420	2.452
Jun-15C	46.886	4.708	15.900	2.607
Dec-15 P	46.100	4.670	16.390	2.767
Dec-15 C	45.836	4.705	16.390	2.766
Jun-16 C	44.865	4.693	16.880	2.932
Dec-16 C	43.889	4.686	17.370	3.102
Jun-17 C	42.922	4.682	17.860	3.277
Dec-17 C	41.986	4.676	18.350	3.457
Jun-18 C	41.049	4.673	18.840	3.640
Dec-18C	40.165	4.665	19.330	3.830
Jun-19 C	39.311	4.658	19.820	4.023
Dec-19 C	38.486	4.648	20.310	4.225
Jun-20 C	37.737	4.632	20.800	4.428
Dec-20 C	36.835	4.638	21.290	4.635
Jun-21 P	36.204	4.612	21.780	4.849
Jun-21 C	36.023	4.635	21.770	4.848
Dec-21 C	35.426	4.608	22.270	5.067
Jun-22 C	34.699	4.599	22.760	5.290
Dec-22 C	34.005	4.587	23.250	5.518
Jun-23C	33.321	4.578	23.740	5.750
Dec-23 C	32.678	4.565	24.230	5.988
Jun-24 C	32.043	4.553	24.720	6.231
Dec-24 C	31.432	4.538	25.220	6.482
Jun-25 C	30.892	4.519	25.710	6.734
Dec-25 C	30.343	4.502	26.200	6.991
Jun-26 C	29.818	4.484	26.690	7.252
Dec-26 C	29.314	4.466	27.180	7.519
Jun-27 C	28.816	4.448	27.670	7.790
Dec-27 C	28.316	4.432	28.160	8.067
Jun-28 C	27.853	4.413	28.650	8.350
Dec-28 C	27.339	4.402	29.140	8.637
Dec-28 P	27.635	4.365	29.150	8.640

(Source: Bloomberg, HSBC)

Appendix II

Volatility

Capital markets operations often contain references to market and instrument *volatility*. Option traders also talk about *implied volatility*. Implied volatility is one of the inputs to the market standard formula used for calculating the price of an option; it cannot be measured directly as it refers to market movements in the future. Historic volatility refers to market movements that have already occurred.

The distribution of asset prices is assumed to follow a lognormal distribution, because the logarithm of the prices is normally distributed (we assume lognormal rather than normal distribution to allow for the fact that prices cannot – as could be the case in a normal distribution – have negative values): the range of possible prices starts at zero and cannot assume a negative value. Returns are defined as the logarithm of the price relatives and are assumed to follow the normal distribution such that:

$$\ln\left(\frac{S_t}{S_0}\right) \sim N\left(\mu t, \sigma\sqrt{t}\right)$$

where

S_0	is the price at time 0
S_t	is the price at time t
$N(m,s)$	is a random variable with mean m and standard deviation s
μ	is the annual rate of return
σ	is the annualised standard deviation of returns

and the symbol ~ means "is distributed according to".

Volatility is defined in the equation above as the annualised standard deviation of returns. This definition does not refer to the variability of the prices directly but to the variability of the returns that generate these prices. Price relatives are calculated from the ratio of successive closing prices. Returns are then calculated according to the following equation as the logarithm of the price relatives:

$$\text{return} = \ln\left(\frac{S_{t+1}}{S_t}\right)$$

where

S_t is the market price at time t
S_{t+1} is the price one period later

The mean and standard deviation of returns follow standard statistical techniques using the following formula:

$$\mu = \sum_{i=I}^{N} \frac{x_i}{N} \quad \text{and} \quad \sigma = \sqrt{\sum_{i=I}^{N} \frac{(x-\mu)^2}{N-1}}$$

where

x_i is the i'th price relative
N is the total number of observations

This gives a standard deviation or volatility of daily price returns. To convert this to annual figure, it is necessary to multiply it by the square root of the number of working days in a year, normally taken to be 250.

* * * *

Selected Bibliography

Bank of England, *The Official Gilt Strips Facility*, October 1997

Bank of England, *Quarterly Bulletin*, February 1998, February 1999

Bierwag, G., *Duration Analysis*, Ballinger 1987

Choudhry, M., *The Bond and Money Markets: Strategy, Trading, Analysis,* Butterworth - Heinemann 2001

Debt Management Office, *The future of UK government cash management*, December 1998

Debt Management Office, *Gilt Review*, 1997–1998

The Economist, *Admiring those shapely curves*, 4 April 1998, p.117

Fabozzi, F., Pollack, I., *Handbook of Fixed Income Securities,* Dow–Jones 1991

Fabozzi, F., *Handbook of US Treasury and Government Agency Securities*, Probus 1990

Grabbe, J., *International Financial Markets*,, Elsevier 2nd ed., 1991

Higson, C., *Business Finance*, Butterworths 1995

Stigum, M., *The Money Market*, Irwin 1990

Wisniewski, M., *Quantitative Methods*, Pitman 1994

Securities Institute Publishing

Each publication provides a detailed overview and practical introduction to key topics within financial services.

The two titles in our *Essential Elements* series – EMU and Money Laundering – provide rapid briefing on key issues as they arise. Each booklet contains the relevant facts and figures to give you an overview of the subject.

Our *Griffin Guide* range consists of re–worked and updated notes from our popular courses. These publications are a useful reference for everyone who needs to grasp the basics of a topic – fast!

To place an order or find out more, call now on *020 7645 0680.*

Essential Elements

Essential Elements of the Prevention of Money Laundering

This quick guide looks at the scale of the problem and efforts taken to overcome it: an essential reference for all who are concerned to identify attempts at money laundering within their organisation.

- What is money laundering?
- Money laundering and the law
- How do you spot it in the process, and what to do.

£4.99 48pp paperback, ISBN: 1 84307 005 7, 2nd edition

The Essential Elements of Economic & Monetary Union

Economic and Monetary Union (EMU) is the system that links together the economies and currencies of the participating European countries. The European Central Bank has become responsible for centralised monetary policy. What does the Euro mean for you?

- Convergence
- Impact of the Euro on the markets
- Preparing for the future.

£4.99 28pp paperback, ISBN: 1 900520 31 1

Griffin Guides

The Fundamentals of CREST

The Fundamentals of CREST gives a detailed overview of securities administration and settlement through the CREST system. It is illustrated throughout with diagrams and tables, bullet points and summaries.

- Handling Certificated Securities
- Corporate Actions and Claims
- Stock Loans and Collateral.

£14.99 128pp paperback, ISBN: 1 900520 98 2
2nd edition

An Introduction to Corporate Finance - Transactions and Techniques

Introduction to Corporate Finance provides readers with the key elements of corporate finance. The book introduces the principle techniques used in corporate finance, combined with practical experience and hands-on, numerically orientated case studies.

- Sources of Capital
- Flotations/Initial Public Offerings
- Mergers and Acquisitions
- Management Buy Outs
- Determining the Cost of Capital
- International Equity Offerings
- Valuing Securities
- Well illustrated with diagrams and tables, bullet points and summaries.

£19.99 96pp paperback, ISBN: 1 900520 09 5

An Introduction to Swaps

An Introduction to Swaps gives a detailed overview of how the various categories of swap work, how they are traded and what they are used for. Topics include interest rate swaps, managing risk, asset swaps, currency swaps. The book is illustrated with over 50 diagrams and tables.

- Managing risk with swaps
- Asset swaps
- Currency swaps.

£19.99 160pp paperback, ISBN: 1 900520 21 4

An Introduction to Fund Management

An Introduction to Fund Management introduces readers to the economic rationale for the existence of funds, the different types available, investment strategies and many other related issues from the perspective of the investment manager. Topics include the features and characteristics of funds, portfolio management and administration, performance measurement and investment mathematics. Includes relevant formulae, equations and examples.

- Features and characteristics of funds
- Portfolio management and administration
- Performance measurement
- Investment mathematics.

£19.99 160pp paperback, ISBN: 1 900520 61 3

An Introduction to Value–at–Risk

An Introduction to Value–at–Risk has been written for those with little or no previous understanding of or exposure to the concepts of risk management and Value–at–Risk. Topics include applications of VaR, instrument structures, stress testing, VaR for corporates, credit risk and legal/regulatory issues.

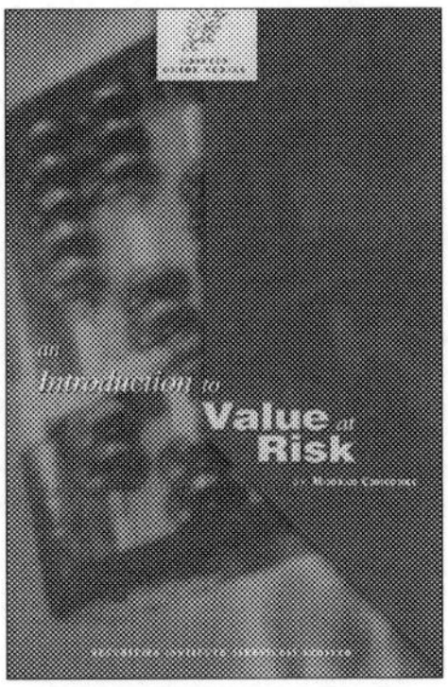

- Risk and Risk management
- VaR and Derivatives, Fixed Interest products.
- VaR for Corporates

£19.99 208pp paperback, ISBN: 1 900520 63 X, 2nd edition

Introduction to Equity Markets

Introduction to Equity Markets provides an overview of the current financial services industry. The book introduces the reader to different types of companies and shares as well as analysis of UK markets. An overview of dealing and settlement in some of the world's major markets is also featured. Contents include:

- Shareholders and Company Law
- Issuing Shares – The Primary Market
- Trading Shares – The Secondary Market
- Settlement of Transactions
- Major Overseas Exchanges and Indices
- Dividends, Bonus Issues and Rights Issues
- Company Accounts.

£19.99 170pp paperback, ISBN: 1 900520 71 0

Introduction to Repo Markets

An Introduction to Repo Markets provides a comprehensive description and analysis of the repo markets. The text has been written to cater for those with little or no previous experience of the repo markets, though it also develops the subject matter to sufficient depth to be of use to more experienced practitioners. Contents include:

- Uses and economic functions of repo
- Accounting, Tax and Capital issues
- The UK gilt repo market
- The implied repo rate and basis trading
- Repo and the yield curve

£19.99 240pp paperback, ISBN: 1 900520 86 9 2nd edition

Introduction to Bond Markets

Introduction to Bond Markets provides a comprehensive, authoritative description and analysis of the bond markets. The book considers basic 'plain vanilla' bonds and elementary bond mathematics, before looking at the array of different instruments available. Contents include:

- Bond Yield Measurement
- Corporate Debt Markets
- Eurobonds
- Introduction to Repo
- Risk Management
- Off–Balance Sheet Instruments
- Government Bond Markets
- Emerging Bond Markets.

£19.99 410pp paperback, ISBN: 1 900520 79 6, 2nd edition